An American Soldier's Saga of the Korean War

by

Former Ambassador and Lt. General (Ret.)
Edward L. Rowny

Edited by

Anne Kazel-Wilcox

Washington, D.C.

Our thanks to these individuals for their great assistance
in the production of this book:

Joanna Rose Williams
David Johns
Michael Crowley
Paul Rowny

Special thanks to
John & Susan Vetter of Freeport, Florida and
John "J-Cat" Griffith of Vista, California
for their kind permission to use some of the photographs in
the list of Medal of Honor recipients.

Cover and interior book design by Victoria Valentine

This book is dedicated to the valorous
members of the armed forces of Korea and
the United Nations who sacrificed for the
freedom of the Republic of Korea.

Contents

Foreword

The following account of my experiences in the Korean War consists of three excerpted chapters from my book: *Smokey Joe and the General* edited by Anne Kazel-Wilcox, which will be published in the summer of 2013. In addition to chapters 17, 18 and 19 relating to Korea, the saga following also contains an epilogue and two brief excerpts from other chapters in the book, along with information on how to order an advance copy of *Smokey Joe and the General*.

Smokey Joe and the General is an account of my life and the remarkable journey I embarked upon under the guidance and inspiration of eccentric but brilliant General John E. Wood. The book commences just prior to America's entrance into World War II and takes the reader through some unforgettable conflicts in modern history, both on the field and off, including the Korean War, Vietnam War, and Cold War. It describes how I helped plan the Inchon invasion, and air-dropped a bridge to Marines and Army soldiers surrounded by Chinese, allowing them to escape from the Chosin reservoir in North Korea. It tells of my success at arming helicopters, overcoming fierce inter-service rivalries. The book takes the reader into the inner sanctums of great military leaders who I worked for directly – Generals Marshall, MacArthur, and Eisenhower, as well as Generals Ridgway, Bradley and Patton. I take the reader behind the scenes at the White House when I worked directly for President Ronald Reagan. Through it all, there are many twists, turns and fastballs. "Smokey Joe Wood," nicknamed after the famous Red Sox pitcher, like him threw not only fast but curveballs.

Smokey Joe and the General begins in 1941 when I was assigned to Colonel Wood's 41st "Singing Engineers" Regiment, so called because it consisted of black soldiers renowned for singing rousing spirituals as they marched. The flamboyant Wood, one of the best trainers in the Army, succeeded in turning misfits into good soldiers.

The book includes a multitude of never-before revealed incidents including the following highlights:

- The WWII scene in Africa with FDR that the press didn't hear about
- The "suicide" mission for US troops in the Italian Campaign in WWII
- The Manhattan engineer that interfered with my plans for the final invasion of Japan
- The conception of "crazy" ideas like sending a man to the moon and shooting ballistic missiles from submarines
- The simple words of a US Secretary of State that unwittingly prompted a Soviet invasion of Korea
- My becoming a spokesman for General MacArthur and how he walked on water

- My account of how the Marine Corps, faced with extinction, was saved by an Army officer working with his Marine Corps VMI classmate.

- A behind-the-scenes look at planning the Inchon Invasion, the "22nd greatest battle of the world"

- How 100,000 North Koreans were saved from certain death when they became "Christmas Cargo," a part of the evacuation of Hungnam

- Smokey Joe's and my assessment of the three top Generals I worked for: Marshall, MacArthur and Eisenhower

- Why when General de Gaulle ordered U.S. troops and supplies out of France I took our golf courses with us

- My story of how my friend Fritz Kraemer discovered and mentored Henry Kissinger, and later kissed him off

- My tale of how I introduced armed helicopters into Vietnam over the objections of the Chief of Naval operations and chiefs of staff of the U.S. Air Force and Army

- My History of how Smokey Joe trained me to take on "impossible" jobs had me promoted ahead of my contemporaries.

To preface the excerpted chapters of my book pertaining to Korea, here is some brief background of how I got into the Korean War (which is detailed in full in Chapter 16 of *Smokey Joe and the General*):

In the fall of 1949, after completing two years of study at Yale, I was rushed to Tokyo for an assignment only to have it postponed for a month. I was given an open ticket to travel around Japan for a month by air, rail and ship and for the next 30 days, visited all the major population centers of Japan. While the purpose of my trip was to get to know Japan, not check on military installations, I couldn't help but notice the failings of our occupational forces. I came away believing there was no need for them given there was no danger of a Japanese military revival.

When I returned from my tour, I wrote a report citing these observations. Colonel Dewitt Armstrong, my division chief, approved my recommendation that our troops be pulled back to training camps for possible deployment elsewhere. The elsewhere I had in mind was, of course, Korea. To replace our forces in Japan, I recommended the formation of a "Japanese Self Defense Force" patterned after the U.S. National Guard. Its mission was to handle civil disorders and natural disasters. The defense force was created and still exists today.

Early in June 1950 I sent a memorandum to my boss, Colonel Armstrong, telling him that from reading intelligence cables, I believed we should be alert to the possibility of North Korea attacking the south. My boss sent the memo to the chief of staff, General Almond, who in turn sent it to the chief of intelligence, General Willoughby, for comments. Willoughby took a dim view of anybody outside his intelligence staff interfering with his business and insisted that the North Koreans would not attack.

That same month, as we were still pulling out troops from villages around Japan, the Korean War broke out. Our troops had been assembled at training camps south of Tokyo, and we quickly formed them into regimental units to deploy to Korea soon after the North attacked.

I now begin the chapter excerpts with Inchon...

17

Invading Inchon

By coincidence, one might say poetic justice, I was the duty officer at MacArthur's headquarters on Sunday, June 25th when the message came in saying that the North Koreans had attacked. I immediately called General Almond who told me to meet him at General MacArthur's apartment. I arrived at MacArthur's luxurious flat, the former residence of a Japanese Zaibatsu industrial magnate, as fast as my driver could navigate the busy streets of Tokyo. Without so much as a hello, General MacArthur asked in a gruff voice, "Rowny, are you going to say 'I told you so?'" I didn't say anything, but must have looked like the cat that swallowed the canary.

38th Parallel in Korea. Sign erected by the 1st Cavalry Division.

THE WAR BEGAN HERE –
JUNE 25, 1950
38TH PARALLEL
COURTESY
1ST CAVALRY DIVISION

General Douglas
MacArthur,
1944.
U.S. GOVERNMENT PHOTO

I was impressed that General MacArthur was quite calm and unperturbed. Being a Sunday, almost everyone had the day off. General MacArthur had Almond order his staff back to work, which included about 500 officers, communicators and support staff in total, everyone necessary to put the Far East Command on war status. MacArthur was on the phone with officials in Seoul and Washington while Almond had the staff prepare follow up messages. All U.S. troops in Japan were ordered to return to barracks immediately.

After our meeting, I disappeared into the recesses of our head-quarters at the seven-story Dai-Ichi building, which was entirely oc-cupied by MacArthur's military and civilian staffs. I barely saw the light of day for the next week. My wife brought me clean clothes and toilet articles while we worked round the clock, taking breaks only for short catnaps on cots.

Our principal contact in Seoul was Ambassador John Muccio, a senior State Department career officer and remarkable individual. He'd been advocating for a year for extra troops and equipment in South Korea, believing the U.S. presence woefully inadequate. De-spite the turmoil he remained confident and in control. As the senior official, he issued instructions to the military that our troops dig in and be prepared to fight.

Back at headquarters a crisis developed in MacArthur's staff. Reporters from the States and other countries arrived almost immediately and were camped out on the press floor of the Dai-Ichi building clamoring for information. The pub-lic relations officer, unable to handle the pressure, reportedly fortified his courage with several stiff drinks and became inco-herent. Later that day, I received a two-line directive from the supreme commander. It read:

1. Effective immediately, you will — in addition to your other du-ties— act as my official spokesman.

2. You will tell the press everything they need know and nothing they need not know.

Signed: Douglas MacArthur

It was a simple, direct order that gave me a great deal of freedom. Why MacArthur chose me, I don't know except that he knew I had intimate knowledge of both the North and South Korean forces and easy access to top staff.

For the next two months, I shed many pounds and nearly lost my sanity dealing with demanding reporters. Among them were the famous Alsop brothers, political journalists from Washington who knew just about everyone of importance.

As I was jousting with journalists, our troops in Korea courageously fought rear-guard actions throughout July but were no match for the enemy. The North Koreans crossed the 38th parallel with 90,000 troops and over 150 Soviet tanks. The Soviets had been protecting their "back door" for several years, strengthening their communist grip in North Korea.

The South Korean troops were poorly trained and badly equipped; only about half had U.S. small arms and we were at the bottom of the priority list for additional supplies.

General MacArthur directed Ambassador Muccio to organize a convoy to take U.S. dependents to Inchon for evacuation to Japan. He ordered Major General William Dean, Commander of the 7th Infantry Division in Japan, to airlift an advance party of the division into Taejon, the large airbase about 100 kilometers south of Seoul.

General Dean and a group of about 550 officers and soldiers landed at Taejon eight days later on July 3. General Dean's instructions were to have the advance party move to the north and when they met our retreating forces, take over command from Ambassador Muccio. Lt. Col. Charles B. Smith, commander of Task Force Smith, met our retreating forces at Osan, about 30 kilometers south of Seoul. Displaying great leadership, he rallied the retreating forces and quickly organized defenses north of Osan. General MacArthur told Dean that Smith should show the enemy "an arrogant display of strength."

U.S. soldiers in
Korea. November
20, 1950.
PHOTO BY PFC. JAMES COX

Smith slowed the enemy's advance by fighting a series of brilliant rear-guard actions. He valiantly pitted his smaller, inferior U.S. Sherman tanks against the powerful Soviet T-34's. Lacking anti-tank weapons, his soldiers bravely infiltrated the enemy's positions at night, attacking their tanks with Molotov cocktails. When the North Korean forces stopped to refuel their vehicles, Smith surprised them by launching counterattacks. On one occasion when he forced the North Koreans to fall back, his men found American prisoners with hands tied behind their backs and shot in the head. Infuriated, they fought even harder. More than one-half of Colonel Smith's forces were killed or wounded. The remainder, feeling they had defended the Alamo, yelled, "No more Task Force Smiths!" Nevertheless, Smith organized them into a coherent fighting force, and they continued to delay the enemy's advance.

After a month of stubbornly defending each kilometer, the South Korean and U.S. forces were driven south to the outskirts of the port of Pusan. Their successful delaying action gave General MacArthur the time he needed to insert the remainder of the 7th Infantry Division from Japan into Pusan. The newly arrived forces allowed the existing ones to build a strong defensive perimeter around Pusan. Supplied with hundreds of thousands of rounds of artillery and provided with air support from Japan, they were able to keep the enemy at bay. The American forces continued to defend the Pusan perimeter throughout the month of August.

There were two schools of thought in General MacArthur's headquarters on what the next step should be. The first and prevailing one was that we should pull our troops out of Korea and evacuate them to Japan, since we lacked sufficient forces for an offensive action. The second, held by General Almond, was to launch an offensive amphibious operation. The problem with his plan was that an amphibious operation would require at least two divisions, about 30,000 troops. Typically, it takes a three-to-one ratio to defeat an entrenched enemy. The North Koreans were defending Seoul with one division but General MacArthur thought two good U.S. divisions were enough to defeat them.

By scraping up additional Army forces from Japan, we were able to strengthen the existing perimeter. This freed up the 7th Division to be available for an amphibious operation. To make up a second division for an invasion, we needed two additional regiments to add to the one regiment of Marines within the perimeter.

General Almond came up with a solution. He invited his VMI classmate, Lieutenant General Lemuel Shepherd, Commander of the Fleet Marine Forces in the Pacific, to Tokyo. Almond knew something most others did not. President Truman had recently ordered the dissolution of all ground forces from the Marine Corps. He felt that the Marines should revert to their original tasks of "protecting the ship's captain from a mutinous crew," and guarding U.S. Embassies abroad. General Ned Almond asked his friend Lem if he could recruit 10,000 Marine reservists to volunteer for active duty. General Shepherd quickly sprang into action and within two weeks signed up the required number to form two additional regiments to fill out the 1st Marine Division. General Shepherd was motivated by the realization that if the Marines participated in a successful invasion, the future of the Marine Corps would be assured.

On July 21, 1950, with the prospect of having the 7th Army Division and 1st Marine Division for an invading force, two other officers and I were instructed to draw up plans for an amphibious invasion. The first, Colonel Lynn Smith, had the reputation of being the best planner in the U.S. Army. The second, Colonel James Landrum, was a distinguished war hero who earned the nation's second highest award, the Distinguished Service Cross, in WWII. Each of us was directed to draw up a plan independent of the others.

We were single-minded in thinking our forces should land on the west coast. Smith picked the classic approach of launching an amphibious attack at the juncture of friendly and enemy forces. Landrum believed we should land farther north, about 10 kilometers behind the front line, which would introduce an element of surprise and still be in range of artillery support. I picked a landing beach some 20 kilometers to the north. That would greatly surprise the enemy since our force would be denied artillery support. I reasoned that we could make up the loss of this artillery fire by the use of air support from Japan. After we presented our plans to General Almond, he decided not to select one but to have us present them to General MacArthur.

MacArthur listened carefully to the first two plans. I was trembling by the time he got to me; he might not think me bold but simply foolish for planning to attack so deep. He surprised us all. Going to a map, he picked up a grease pencil and drew a big arrow more than 350 kilometers up the west coast — right through Inchon opposite Seoul.

"Always go for the objective," said MacArthur, "and the objective is Seoul."

To MacArthur, recapturing the capital would be immensely symbolic.

"You're all pusillanimous," he said. I did not know the meaning of pusillanimous but from the tone of his voice I guessed it was nothing complimentary. "Why not terrain-hop and land at Inchon?" he said. "Have you considered that?"

MacArthur learned during the Pacific war that the best way to succeed was by island hopping and this would be a similar maneuver.

"Yes, general, we thought about it," I said. "But there are several good reasons against it. First, it's very close to Seoul and the enemy would certainly defend the capital in great strength. Second, it's the most difficult of all places for a landing because the tides are so huge. Inchon has a 32-foot tide, the second greatest tidal range in the world. It would be difficult for a landing force to fight without reinforcements until they could arrive on the next tide.

MacArthur said simply: "Go for the throat, the tides are simply another obstacle to be overcome." Quoting Andrew Jackson he said, "Never take counsel of your fears."

Smith, Landrum and I combined forces and drew up the plan to invade Inchon. But it still had to pass muster in Washington. The Pentagon preferred a "Dunkirk" operation, evacuating our troops to Japan. MacArthur thought that an evacuation would lower troop morale and undermine U.S confidence in him.

The Joint Chiefs of Staff thought Inchon the worst place for an amphibious landing. The high tides and the 30-foot walls surrounding the port made a landing extremely difficult. Undeterred, MacArthur invited them to Tokyo to outline the details of our plan. He had us outline the plan, after which the chief of the Air Force spoke first. He said it was unnecessary to land troops amphibiously. "Give me a sufficient number of bombs, and I will so heavily damage the enemy's supply lines that they will have to pull back."

He was followed by the chief of Naval operations.

"A 32-foot tide," he said, "makes an amphibious landing impossible. We cannot land a sufficient number of troops on the beach before the tide turns. Besides, the area is heavily sown with powerful sea mines and underwater obstacles."

Finally, the chief of staff of the Army objected to the landing site because it would be where the enemy would defend the capital of Seoul most strongly. He thought our two-division force would not be strong enough to prevail. The chairman of the Joint Chiefs of Staff, General Lawton Collins, remained silent. He knew MacArthur well and hesitated to take him on.

General MacArthur then took the floor. Crisply and elegantly, often citing examples from the Peloponnesian Wars and other classic battles, he charmed the chiefs with a six-hour histrionic performance. Halfway through the theatrics, in walked his aide, Second Lieutenant Alexander Haig, ostensibly to serve sandwiches but probably more desirous of his 15 minutes of fame amidst 25 stars. MacArthur's lecture was a tour de force that I thought outdid John Barrymore.

When he finished, General Collins said, "I think we all approve, don't we?" The other chiefs were too intimidated to object.

The next day, MacArthur called us into his office, one at a time. When I entered, MacArthur gave me a bear hug and said, "Colonel Rowny, Inchon will go down in history as the 22nd great battle of the world." At West Point, I had often studied the 70-foot mural in our dining hall depicting British historian Creasey's 15 great battles of the world from Marathon to Waterloo. There is a broad consensus among historians that there were five great battles since, the last two being Stalingrad and Normandy.

Edward Rowny, Korea, 1950.
ROWNY PHOTO COLLECTION

"What was the 21st?" I asked General MacArthur.

"The Battle of Warsaw in 1920," he said, "where Polish Marshal Josef Pilsudski' stopped the Bolsheviks from capturing Warsaw. Had the Polish capital fallen, the communists would have overrun Western Europe."

Creasey's criterion for qualifying as a great battle was whether a different outcome would have meant the end of western civilization as we know it. Amazed by General MacArthur's great historical knowledge, I, too, hoped Inchon would go down in history as the 22nd great battle of the world. Not having time to reflect further, MacArthur pumped my hand and I came back to earth still feeling eight feet tall.

I told my wife about the meeting that evening, saying: "I believe he can put on his trousers two legs at a time. I am certain he can walk on water."

The next day, Colonels Smith, Landrum and I combined forces to plan for the Inchon invasion. We decided that the Marine Division would be the first to land. It would be followed by the 7th Infantry Division. Once the two divisions secured a foothold, we would bring ashore the heavy artillery, engineers and other supporting troops.

The two divisions and supporting troops were placed under a newly constituted X Corps. General MacArthur had supreme confidence in his Chief of Staff and promoted General Edward Almond to three star rank as commander of X Corps. Under normal circumstances, the X Corps would have been placed under General Walton Walker, Commanding General of the Eighth U.S. Army, to whom all United States forces in the Far East belonged. However, MacArthur took the unprecedented step of having Almond report directly to him. The primary reason for this unusual act was the loss of MacArthur's confidence in General Walker. He thought the general should have been more aggressive in relieving Army forces in Japan of their occupation duties, and should have trained the officers and men of the reconstituted Eighth Army more rigorously. Adding further injury to the insult, General MacArthur retained Almond as his Chief of Staff so that General Walker would not only be denied command of a key unit but have MacArthur's orders issued to him through his principal staff officer. It was no overstatement that there was no love lost between the Eighth Army and X Corps commanders, Walker believing that Almond had poisoned MacArthur's mind against him.

The first problem requiring a decision for the invasion was that of timing. After consulting the chart of tides and the historical record of typhoons, we sent our analysis and recommendation to General Almond that the invasion take place on the 15th of September. That date had a combination of favorable tides, good weather and the least historical probability of a typhoon. Mid-September would allow scarcely enough time to assemble the necessary troops and equipment but waiting for the next favorable tides was not an option; a month later would bump us up against the dead of winter in an area known for inhospitable sub-zero temperatures.

It took only hours for us to learn the decision. It read: "Good work. Approved – Almond."

The next decision was whether to invade from small boats or LSTs. The advantage of small boats was that it would disperse the landing force, making it less vulnerable to enemy artillery and mortar fires. The disadvantage was that small, squad-sized units would not be strong enough to attack fortified positions. LSTs offered the advantage of an entire company, together with its supporting weapons and ammunition, being able to land as a single unit. However, once an LST hit the beach, troops and equipment had to unload quickly, leaving it like a beached whale, vulnerable to enemy attacks for the next 12 hours until the tide changed. Clearly, LSTs were the way to go — strength in numbers. Nevertheless, a large obstacle remained. Although we had sufficient LSTs in mothballs, we did not have enough captains to steer them. Japan had available LST pilots but the Japanese government, fearful of Soviet reprisals, was reluctant to allow us to hire them. Officials relented after we promised to keep the information classified. Here again, the chief of staff approved and sent us a note: "That's the way to go, Almond."

General MacArthur let us know that he wanted to triumphantly return President Syngman Rhee to Seoul on September 29, a date of great symbolic importance since it marked three months since Seoul fell. The general would not countenance entering Seoul with President Rhee by helicopter or landing on the shore south of Seoul in amtracs. He insisted on a motorcade to enter Seoul via a bridge over the Han.

Short of that, MacArthur believed public opinion would not accept that the Korean capital was securely in our hands.

September 29th, however, was a scant two weeks after the invasion and we were certain that the North Koreans would destroy the only bridge crossing the Han before we could seize it. Accordingly, the next job I tackled was assembling bridging to span the river. This proved difficult since there was not sufficient bridging of a single type in the entire Pacific theatre. The normal amount of bridging stored in any one place would only cross a river 350-meters wide, and the Han River along our route from Inchon to Seoul was over a kilometer in width. Only by using three different types of bridges — 50 pontoons in all — could we amass what we needed and even then there was no standardized linking system between the different types. That necessitated planning to set up forge shops to manufacture connectors after the landing. On top of that, the Han was a tidal river with strong currents of six miles per hour, among the world's fastest rivers, and the current reversed every 12 hours. So while each pontoon had an anchor, we needed 50 more to anchor the other side of each pontoon for stability when the tide reversed. Coming up with that many extra anchors was not as simple as it would seem.

Syngman Rhee with Rear Admiral Ralph A. Ofstie, U.S. Navy, receiving the Republic of Korea's Order of Military Merit, May 13, 1952.
U.S. NAVY PHOTO

As the only engineer in our planning group, it was my job to plan for the river crossing. Looking over my shoulder, General MacArthur said, "Rowny, you appear to know how to build a bridge and I want you to be the X Corps engineer."

13

"I can't do that, sir," I replied. "A Corps engineer is a brigadier general and I'm only a lieutenant colonel."

"No problem," said the general. "I'm promoting you to the rank of brigadier general effective immediately."

What MacArthur wanted, he got. He advanced me to "brevet" brigadier general, meaning I would wear a star for as long as MacArthur wanted me in that position, and with it came all the privileges and authority of a brigadier general — but not the pay. I was quite proud since the only officer I knew who was brevetted a brigadier general was my hero, Thaddeus Kosciusko, George Washington's engineer during the Revolutionary War.

There were more obstacles to overcome. To enable our troops to mount the 30-foot high walls that surrounded the port of Inchon, we ordered the construction of 200 aluminum ladders from Japanese factories, with each built in 10-foot sections so that three could be assembled together to scale the walls. Placing this order was a dead giveaway that we were planning an invasion, which reporters could have easily figured out was to take place at Inchon, the only South Korean port heavily fortified by a seawall. Yet reporters did not divulge what they knew. We thanked God that the media knew how to keep a secret.

Drinking water was another major concern. Intelligence sources told us that the water supply at Inchon was brackish, and a single pipeline from Seoul supplied the only potable water. The North Koreans could simply turn off the line at Seoul and dry us up, or at least that's what we would do to deter an invading force. Our solution was to carry fresh water in tankers, but the only tankers available in the Pacific Theater were vessels that transported oil. Despite three steam cleanings, we couldn't get rid of the oil slicks on the water. We knew the water would make our troops sick but had no alternative than to go with those tankers. As it turned out, the North Koreans didn't know we had a potential problem and neglected to turn off the fresh water supply.

There were many other logistical problems to overcome in gathering the troops and equipment and getting them moving in a short period of time. Numerous supplies were needed from the Japan, Hawaii and the Western U.S.

We managed to overcome these obstacles but faced a major storm two days before the planned landing. We were devastated when a substantial portion of bridge material was swept overboard. Taking inventory, we found we lacked an astounding eight tons of material. I put in an urgent request to locate the necessary bridging on the West Coast of the U.S. and have it flown into Kimpo Airfield after we invaded Inchon. The airfield was an important U.S. objective between Inchon and Seoul. My request was contentious because airlifts into Kimpo were earmarked for priority items such as machine gun, mortar and artillery ammunition. Nevertheless, I got the airlift approved.

The 14th of September was a long day I thought would never end. For no good reason other than our nervousness, General Almond and our entire staff of the X Corps arose before dawn aboard U.S.S. Mount McKinley. Instead of waiting for the meeting scheduled for 9 a.m., we all drifted into the boardroom two hours earlier and by 9 a.m. had rehearsed what we would do the next day, D-Day. We drank endless cups of coffee, worried and prayed. The flowing adrenaline and caffeine gave us short highs and long lows. We worried whether our invasion had been detected and if we would soon be strafed by North Korean planes based at Kimpo.

No air attacks came, but instead of calming us, we only grew more anxious. We fretted over striking one of the hundreds of floating and sunken mines which intelligence officers told us were protecting Inchon. We worried whether the North Koreans were dispatching troops from north of the Han to defend Inchon's harbor walls and beaches. At noon, the galley was empty since most of us were not interested in food. Repeating our morning pattern, we drifted into the boardroom at 1 p.m. for the church service scheduled to begin two hours later. The chaplain was delighted since he had only been allotted 45 minutes for the service but now had two hours to conduct a Baptist revival. It was my first service of this kind, and I found myself clapping and shouting, "Praise the Lord" and "Amen." Thoroughly exhausted, we hit our bunks after the sun went down but for most, it was a sleepless night that would end with 5:00 a.m. reveille.

Inchon Landing, September 15, 1950.
PHOTO BY U.S. NAVY

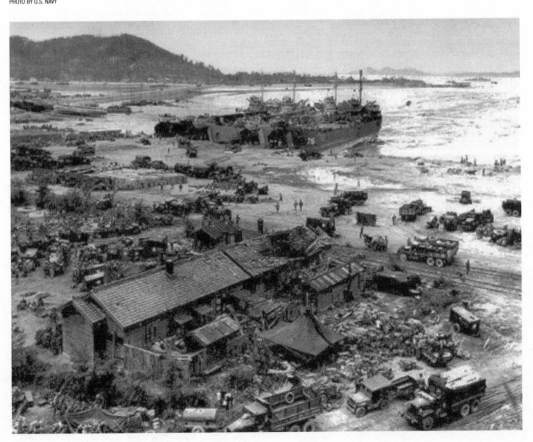

The invasion commenced shortly after dawn on September 15, 1950, at high tide. About 1,000 Marines of the 1st Regiment stormed ashore from LSTs. They began scaling the walls, climbing up the 200 aluminum ladders and charging over the impenetrable walls of Inchon. The remaining 2,000 troops from that regiment landed on the beach on the northern side of the wall. The 5th Marine Regiment, about 3,000-strong, landed south of the wall. This

Inchon Landing, U.S. Marines, September 15, 1950.
U.S. MARINE CORPS PHOTO

first wave quickly dispatched the North Korean defenders and suffered only light casualties. By the time the water receded, the Marines were well established ashore. The second wave rode in 12 hours later with the dusk high tide. LSTs unloaded vehicles, tanks, and light artillery pieces and then lay high and dry until the incoming tide permitted their return.

We achieved complete surprise and the invasion was a resounding success. Despite the anticipated obstacles, we were fortunate. Mines and underwater obstacles were non-existent. Furthermore, enemy resistance was light. It was a great relief to those of us who had planned the invasion and participated in the first wave. We recalled that General MacArthur believed that if planners had to land in the first wave of an invasion it would sharpen their minds. He was right and we were lucky.

By the completion of the third wave the next morning, all of the Marines and most of their equipment had landed, and the troops were fighting their way against moderate resistance toward Seoul. General Almond decided to come ashore with his G-3, Colonel McCaffrey, and invited me to join them. We briefly visited two of the regimental commanders of the 1st Marine Division. The first, Colonel Lewis "Chesty" Puller, a highly decorated Marine officer, had earned two Distinguished Navy Crosses. The second, Colonel Raymond "Ray" Murray, although shot in the leg, insisted on retaining command while on crutches.

Puller's outfit had advanced farther than Murray's, about two kilometers from the beach. General Almond complimented him and asked why he was not continuing to advance towards the Han since enemy resistance was not strong. Puller said he was awaiting orders from his division commander, Major General Oliver P. Smith, before advancing.

"Marine doctrine," he added, "holds that after landing, troops must wait until all artillery is ashore before advancing."

While the light artillery had come ashore, the heavy artillery was still at sea.

"I don't give a fig for Marine doctrine," said Almond. "Unless you move out smartly, the enemy will bring in reinforcements and the Han will be harder to cross."

"Sir, I'm sorry," said Puller, "But I only take orders through the chain of command."

General Almond called the Marines' commanding general on the radio.

"General Smith," he said, "I would like you to order Colonels Puller and Murray to advance to the north."

"I can't do that," replied Smith, "Marine Corps doctrine states that we're not to advance until all the artillery is ashore."

Almond patiently explained that there were times to forget doctrine and this was one of those times. Smith was unmoved.

"I'm going to turn my radio over to Colonel Puller and I want you to order him to move to the north," Almond said.

Smith did. With a big smile on his face, Puller, anxious to be unleashed, saluted General Almond and said, "Here we go."

Puller understood the need to advance rapidly and was anxious to do so.

By this time enemy resistance stiffened. The Marines were faced with a counterattack by a column of North Korean tanks, which had crossed the river. Chesty Puller called for air support, which responded magnificently. Within an hour, our planes swooped down and took out the entire column of enemy tanks. Almond kept pushing the Marines to move rapidly, insisting that they reach the near side of the Han quickly.

He told the regimental commanders: "Get going and capture the river bank. Don't let the North Koreans build up a force south of the Han."

At the same time, General Smith still at sea, attempted to slow the Marines' advance. The regimental commanders listened to Almond and not Smith.

Advancing toward the river, we learned the North Koreans had already crossed to the south bank and had destroyed the only bridge spanning the Han. This meant that we had to take out pockets of North Koreans south of the Han in order to establish positions from which we could launch an assault across the river.

On September 20, Colonel Murray's 1st Battalion lucked into finding an undefended position and quickly landed on the north side of the Han. It advanced rapidly against light resistance and took up a position west of Seoul.

To the east of Murray's regiment, Chesty Puller, facing stiffer resistance, advanced to Yong Dong Po, south of the Han. He began fortifying the hilltop village, anticipating an attack. Almond paid him a visit saying he wanted to present him with a Silver Star. Approaching Puller, who was crouched down, he asked, "Chesty, why are you crouching down there?"

"I'm not crouching, sir; I'm just playing it safe," answered Puller. "By standing up there, you're drawing fire in on us."

"Don't worry; we're pretty much out of range. What's coming in are spent bullets."

"General, I lost a brother to one of those spent bullets."

Tugging him from his crouched position, Puller got the general to kneel down.

There, hunched over, Almond declared, "I want to present you with a Silver Star for your gallantry in action. Stand up and salute me while we get a photo of me pinning the medal on you."

Puller stood up and as soon as a photographer snapped a photo, he snatched the medal from Almond's hand. Resuming his crouch position, Chesty pulled Almond down beside him and said, "General, you can dispense with reading the citation. I can read it later." He added, "Let's be sensible and talk things over."

Colonel Murray was faced with a situation of having one battalion north of the Han and two south of the river. The enemy reinforced their troops on the northern bank and was encircling Murray's battalion west of Seoul. That night, Colonel Murray had volunteers swim across the Han in the darkness to reconnoiter a river crossing for his two battalions south of the Han. Unfortunately they were spotted and prevented by heavy enemy fire from reaching land. Most of the brave volunteers perished.

Colonel Murray came to me with a problem. "General Rowny," he said, "I don't know how to make a river crossing. At Quantico, we learned how to storm a beach but were never taught how to make an attack across a river."

Incredulous, I explained that in making an invasion you have Marines go down rope ladders from a ship a half-mile or more from shore into amtracs, and fire rockets and machine guns to gain a foothold on the beach. In a river crossing, you load Marines into amtracs on the near shore, and blazing away, attack the far shore. If the crossing is on a tidal river, the amtracs need to be launched from a point down or upstream from the target, calculating in three variables: the speed of the tide, the speed of the amtrac and the distance to be crossed. A river crossing might use smoke screens, as with an invasion, to hamper visibility of the amtracs. In a river crossing you often stage a diversionary attack up or down stream in an attempt to deceive the enemy as to the location of main attack.

Since Colonel Murray felt that he could not properly explain all of this to his junior commanders, I decided to conduct a 101 course in "River Crossing" at Kimpo airfield and had Murray's battalion and company commanders attend. After about an hour, they became comfortable, now knowing what to do.

That evening, Colonel Murray successfully carried out what he and his subordinates learned about river crossings at Kimpo, making a diversionary attack with a platoon. Murray's two battalions successfully crossed the Han. Under cover of a smoke screen and with a heavy artillery bombardment, his troops overcame the enemy defending the north side of the river and secured a foothold. Advancing rapidly against light resistance, Murray's second and third battalions came to the rescue of his beleaguered 1st battalion. His regiment was now securely located west of Seoul.

To the east, a large force of about 5,000 North Koreans crossed the Han and attacked Colonel Puller's forces at dawn. The courageous Marines switched from defense to offense and counterattacked the North Korean invaders. They were successful, and the few surviving enemy were forced to swim back across the Han.

Colonel Puller took advantage of the situation and quickly crossed the Han with his entire regiment. They advanced against light resistance to the eastern side of Seoul. The Marines now had a regiment on either side of Seoul.

Although the Marines were now established in the suburbs east and west of Seoul, they had difficulty capturing the capital. The enemy occupied a strategic hill east of the city and was raining fires down upon them. The hill was called South Mountain by the South Koreans, a tongue-in-cheek reference to the fact that their highest hill was only 494 meters, while the North Koreans had mountains 10,000 meters and higher. General Almond knew it was necessary to take the hill in order to capture Seoul and charged the 32nd Infantry Regiment, which had come ashore with the 7th U.S. Army Division, with the task.

The 32nd Infantry moved to the south bank of the Han opposite their objective to begin preparation for the river crossing. The crossing was to be made in light plastic boats carrying a squad of 12 men propelled by a five-horsepower outboard motor and equipped with a 30-caliber machine gun. The boats, however, were designed to cross rivers with currents of one to two miles per hour. As soon as the boats were shoved into the water the fast currents —about three times stronger — pushed them back ashore. The Army's standard equipment was not going to work.

Crossing in amtracs was the obvious solution. The Marine Corps, which specialized in amphibious warfare, designed the landing craft to ferry weapons and ammunition from ship to shore. The amtrac weighed 17 tons and was equipped with a 250-horespower engine capable of achieving speeds of 7 knots on water and 20 miles per hour on land. Early in WWII, the Marines adapted it as a troop-assault vehicle that carried a platoon of 30 men and was armed with two 50-caliber machine guns. Each Marine division was equipped with 20 amtracs.

General Almond ordered General Smith to turn his division's amtracs over to the 32nd Infantry. Smith refused, saying that the amtracs were Marine Corps property. Thoroughly exasperated, Almond patiently and diplomatically reminded Smith that all military equipment belonged to the U.S. government and furthermore, the 1st Marine Division was part of his X Corps. When Smith again refused, Almond simply commandeered them.

Crossing in amtracs, the 32nd Infantry succeeded in gaining a foothold on the far bank of the Han, suffering only light casualties and losing not a single amtrac. The amtracs returned to the near shore and in a second wave, ferried the regiment's light artillery and a battalion of the division's heavy artillery across the Han. As soon as the artillery pieces were in place, they launched a heavy bombardment on South Mountain. One battalion of the 32nd Infantry attacked from the east and a second from the west, assaulting the hill in a pincer maneuver. Experiencing moderate casualties, the 32nd Infantry captured its objective. With the hill in friendly hands, the Marines were able to execute their own pincer maneuver against Seoul.

Realizing that the jig was up, the enemy fled to the north and the Marines began marching unopposed into the capital. Even before the city fell, however, General MacArthur announced prematurely that Seoul was in U.S. hands. Always seeking a headline, he wanted to dramatize that we had captured the capital on September 25, three months after the North Koreans invaded Seoul.

Meanwhile, I was busy preparing to build the pontoon bridge across the Han, which I planned for the river's narrowest point where the fixed bridge had been destroyed. Constructing the bridge at the narrowest point meant using fewer pontoons and anchors but it was more difficult because here, the water flowed swiftest. We set up forges at Kimpo Airfield where soldiers who had some experience as blacksmiths fashioned connectors for the different types of bridging. It was not an easy job but in two days we produced a sufficient number of fasteners needed for the bridge. Once we had enough connectors, we put the bridge together in the river adjacent to the south bank. Our plan was to anchor one end of the bridge to the near shore and, using two amtracs, swing the other end to the far shore.

We got ready to do this, knowing full well that the North Koreans still had artillery and mortars in place that could fire on us. Army doctrine holds that building a bridge is never begun until the far shore is cleared of all weapons. However, we were under immense pressure from General MacArthur to complete the bridge so that his motor convoy could enter Seoul on his chosen anniversary date: September 29. This date was a scant two weeks after our landing at Inchon. The enemy discovered our plan soon after we got started, and began shelling the bridge with mortar and artillery fire. We continued placing anchors for each pontoon first on one side and then the other so that when the tides reversed the bridge would stay in place.

The enemy shelling of the bridge intensified killing or wounding a number of engineers installing the anchors. Among the fatalities was one of the five engineer colonels under my command who was personally supervising work on the bridge. Another colonel suffered a nervous breakdown, distraught at the thought of being responsible for the death of men building the bridge under fire.

Unknown to those of us at the front, the general's desire for a ceremony in Seoul, which would hand power back to Rhee, was causing high drama in Washington. The State Department thought that turning South Korea over to Rhee was a bad idea because in some circles, he was considered an autocratic dictator. The State Department thought the decision should be left to the United Nations. General MacArthur disagreed, arguing that Rhee was the duly elected president of South Korea. If we did not return him to power, chaos would ensue, he said, and there would be no telling who might end up in power. He felt it was his duty to allow Rhee to carry out his constitutional responsibilities. As usual, what MacArthur wanted, he got.

As this saga was playing out in Washington, we worked round the clock to complete our bridge. One of the colonels under my command, Leigh Fairbanks, proved to be an invaluable asset. I had served under him in the 41st Engineers, and we were together in capturing General Devers in his pajamas. After WWII, Fairbanks pioneered the development of powerful five-foot diameter searchlights that, for the first time, permitted attacks despite no illuminating moon and made it possible to build bridges after dark. Colonel Fairbanks had insisted on these searchlights along with generators for the Han, and they doubled the amount of time we could work on the bridge.

Our work was proceeding smoothly, when on September 28, we suffered a setback. A heavy squall caused several pontoons to break loose from their anchors and drift downstream. It took hours

using amtracs to capture the dislodged pontoons and return them to their former positions. As dawn broke the next day, we succeeded in repairing the damaged bridge using spools of bailing wire to reinforce the connections. We still needed another five hours to complete the bridge when word arrived that MacArthur expected to cross the bridge with President Rhee in a mere two hours.

Through the superhuman effort of our engineers, we made the deadline. General MacArthur and President Rhee landed at Kimpo Airfield, formed a motorcade that was four-Chevrolets and 40-jeeps long and crossed the Han on schedule. Little did they realize that the bridge had only been completed less than an hour earlier. I later wrote my wife that, in those tense moments, I truly wished that MacArthur could walk on water.

The smiles of the military and political leaders turned into somber frowns when they approached the blackened city of Seoul,

Left: After the invasion of Inchon, a South Korean child, September 16, 1950.
PHOTO BY RONALD L. HANCOCK, U.S. ARMY

Below: The rubble of Seoul, November 1, 1950.
PHOTO BY CAPT. F. L. SCHEIBER, U.S. ARMY

which was still ablaze. The procession nonetheless continued on to a damaged auditorium in the capital, where a stirring ceremony took place. Every seat of the auditorium was occupied by senior U.S. officers who had taken part in the invasion, along with the South Korean military and members of Rhee's government.

General MacArthur and President Rhee both spoke eloquently. The general completed his speech by invoking divine will and reciting the Lord's Prayer. Halfway through, a stray shell struck the glass skylight of the auditorium and shards tumbled down. Those with steel helmets quickly donned them. Unperturbed, as though nothing happened, General MacArthur in a clear, loud voice completed his prayer. President Rhee thanked MacArthur and the United Nations for liberating Seoul and placing him back in control. Like MacArthur, he thanked Almighty God for the liberation of Korea. During the ceremony, many in the audience openly wept.

From the time of my arrival in Tokyo until we left for the invasion, I kept up my correspondence with General Wood. He had started his second career as a town planner and wrote me about his innovative and at times eccentric approaches to solving problems. In civilian life, as in the military, it was vintage Smokey Joe. I, in turn, wrote him about my premature arrival in Tokyo and trip around Japan. Wood said the opportunity to travel was fortunate, since it gave me a good grounding in the demography and social mores of the Japanese. He was pleased that General Almond was General MacArthur's chief of staff and not surprised that Almond's regard for MacArthur amounted to hero worship. I said that Almond considered MacArthur the best American general and ranked him among the world's greatest military leaders such as Caesar, Hannibal, and Napoleon. Wood thought this a bit much, but said that even before Almond worked for the general, he called MacArthur a military genius who could do no wrong. General Wood was not surprised that General Almond recruited me to work for him and flattered me by saying that Almond liked to surround himself with talented officers because they advanced his career.

Wood sympathized with my being assigned the onerous job of General MacArthur's spokesman, but thought it a good opportunity to learn how to deal with the press. As for the Inchon invasion, he was delighted that I was chosen as one of the planners. Only a man of MacArthur's erudition, patience and charm, he wrote, could have gotten the Joint Chiefs of Staff to approve the plan. He agreed with MacArthur that Inchon would someday rank as the 22nd great battle of the world. He also commended General MacArthur for his good judgment in making me the engineer of X Corps and brevetting me to the rank of brigadier general, two grades above my rank. Wood reminded me that in my first efficiency report on me, he wrote: "This second lieutenant has the potential to be a general officer and should be promoted to that rank as soon as possible."

More surprising to Wood was that Colonel Fairbanks, his plans and operations officer in the 41st Engineers now led an engineer regiment under my command. But, Wood said, Fairbanks was a true officer and gentleman who could be expected to serve loyally and gracefully even under an officer who was a second lieutenant when he was a captain. Wood speculated that by preaching innovation to his staff, he might have been responsible for Fairbanks having invented the five-foot searchlight.

While Wood approved of General MacArthur's assignment of Almond as X Corps commander, he disapproved of MacArthur's allowing Almond to simultaneously keep his job as chief of staff. I explained that MacArthur had lost confidence in his Eighth Army commander, General Walton Walker and that his double-hatting

Almond made sense. Wood disagreed saying that if MacArthur lost confidence in Walker, he should have relieved him. He was adamant in adhering to the principle of war: unity of command. "No battle can be won", he said, "If not fought under a single commander." However, he wrote that MacArthur is probably the only general who can violate a principle of war — and get away with it.

18 | To the Yalu and Back

Before VJ Day, General Marshall had the staff make plans for the surrender of enemy forces including those in Korea. He instructed my boss, General Abe Lincoln, his chief war planner, to make a recommendation on where to divide North from South Korea following the war. Lincoln assembled the strategic plan division (SPD) in his conference room and asked our opinions. Colonel Dean Rusk spoke first. He said it should be drawn at the 39th parallel north latitude, just south of the city of Pyongyang, the North Korean capital. The 39th was where the Korean Peninsula was narrowest. Fewer U.S. troops would be needed at the "wasp-waist" to defend the border.

"No, no" said Lincoln, who picked up a grease pencil and drew a line on the map at the 38th parallel. "That's where the line should be," he said.

We were all puzzled and Colonel Andy Goodpaster asked Lincoln, "Why go one degree south when the 39th parallel is the obvious solution?"

"Because of Nicholas Spykman," said Lincoln.

Spykman was a Yale geography professor and America's leading "geopolitician." He wrote a book in 1944 called *The Geography of Peace*, in which he held that "Geography is the most fundamental factor in foreign policy because it is the most permanent." He taught in his classes that 90 percent of the world's best literature and inventions were created, and most of the world's great leaders were born, north of the 38th parallel. The remaining 10 percent were south of it.

Showing off his erudition, Lincoln said, "Everyone knows about the 38th parallel but no one has heard of the 39th." In truth, few except intellectual eggheads had ever heard of Spykman, let alone read his work.

We all objected but out of deference to Lincoln, did not go over his head to General Marshall. In retrospect, we should have, because defending the 39th parallel would have been easier, might have been acceptable to the Soviets, and might have saved U.S. lives. Such are the bizarre twists and turns of decision-making.

The weeks following the capture of Seoul were characterized by indecisiveness in Washington. As the mop-up of Seoul neared completion, the Joint Chiefs of Staff sent a message to General MacArthur. It added that actions north of the 38th parallel were authorized as long as there was no evident Chinese or Soviet threat. It further specified that no incursions across the Soviet and Chinese borders or the attacking of targets in those areas with air or naval fire would be allowed. It concluded with the statement: "As a matter of policy, no non-Korean ground forces will be used in the northeast provinces bordering the Soviet Union or in the area along the Manchurian border."

This message made it clear that no U.N. forces, including the U.S., could advance beyond the 38th parallel. Beyond that, only

Retreat of United Nations Forces at 38th parallel, 1950.

forces from the Republic of Korea (ROK) would be authorized to proceed.

Later that day, General Marshall, who had recently been appointed Secretary of Defense, sent General MacArthur a message saying: "We want you to feel unhampered tactically and strategically to proceed north of the 38th parallel."

MacArthur chose to interpret Marshall's message as superseding the earlier message from the Joint Chiefs of Staff and believed he was now authorized to move U.N. forces north of the 38th parallel. Historians to this day debate whether MacArthur should have followed the instructions from the Joint Chiefs or from Marshall. Marshall's instructions may have been intended to supersede those of the Joint Chiefs, or he may have not known of their instructions. Two points are evident: First, the confusion of messages from Washington reflected that there were two schools of thought on how to proceed. Second, MacArthur elected to follow Marshall's later instructions because they authorized him to do what he wanted to do all along.

In mid-October, President Truman met with General MacArthur at Wake Island, halfway between Hawaii and Japan. The meeting lasted only two hours. During the first half-hour the president and the general met alone and no records were kept. One reporter, Merle Miller, wrote about the meeting, saying that General MacArthur kept President Truman waiting, did not salute him, and was otherwise disrespectful. I later heard from Merriman Smith, dean of the White House reporters, that the story was not true. He said the general acted in an entirely respectful manner. Miller was apparently looking to sensationalize the meeting; other historians have since discounted his version of events. Unfortunately, the fabricated account prevails in the press to this day. Years later, however, President Truman wrote in his memoirs that General MacArthur apologized to him for writing to the Veterans of Foreign Wars and for criticizing him. Truman wrote that he accepted MacArthur's apology and told him the subject was closed.

Upon General MacArthur's return to Tokyo following the Wake Island meeting, he ordered FECOM to prepare plans for resuming the fight. Heading up from Inchon, the Eighth U.S. Army's I and IX Corps would serve as the western flank and attack to the north. On the eastern flank, X Corps would make an amphibious landing at Wonsan and then attack north. ROK forces would advance on high ground in the rugged mountains between the two U.S. prongs.

On October 19, 1950, elements of the Eighth Army easily captured Pyongyang as North Korean forces scrambled to disappear into the mountains. ROK forces moved rapidly up the east coast and cap-

Above: Marilyn Monroe, Korea, February 17, 1954. PHOTO BY CPL. WELSHMAN, U.S. ARMY

Right: Bob Hope, Womsan Korea, October 26, 1950. PHOTO BY CPL. ALEX KLEIN, U.S. ARMY

tured Wonsan, making the amphibious landing by X Corps unnecessary. This was fortuitous since the landing would have been nearly impossible due to the large number of Soviet sea mines in the area. The Marines scheduled to make the landing were instead transported from their ships to Wonsan via helicopters. Bob Hope, who had landed with his USO group to entertain X Corps at Wonsan, put up a large sign at the port, which read: "Welcome ashore leathernecks — Bob Hope." Further north, the 7th U.S. Infantry Division of X Corps was airlifted from the Western part of Korea to Hamhung, a city adjoining the port of Hungnam on east coast of North Korea.

A month earlier, there had been reports that Chinese troops were south of the Yalu River, the river that divides North Korea from China. General MacArthur ordered all forces to proceed as rapidly as possible toward the border. As one ROK division in the center advanced, it ran into Chinese forces that virtually destroyed it. Several days later, a second ROK division ran into a superior Chinese force that pinned it down 40 kilometers south of the Yalu. Meanwhile, in

South Korean
soldiers, Suwon
Airfield.
U.S. MILITARY PHOTO

the west, at the Chongchon River, the 7th U.S. cavalry regiment lost 600 of its 900 men and most of its vehicles when it was struck by a superior Chinese force. The cavalry regiment fought tooth and nail to prevent the remaining 300 troopers from being overrun.

On the eastern flank, the 7th captured two Chinese soldiers. The prisoners were brought to X Corps headquarters for interrogation. Since General Willoughby, the Eighth Army intelligence chief doubted that there were Chinese south of the Yalu, General Almond invited him to fly from Tokyo to see for himself.

When Willoughby saw them he said, "They're not Chinese, they're North Korean."

I spoke up saying, "They are definitely Chinese. You can tell by the epicanthic fold of their eyes."

"Don't give me that scientific jazz," said Willoughby. "They're Koreans."

Like many new to the area, Willoughby thought all Asiatics looked the same.

At the end of October General Almond assembled the three divisions of the X Corps — 1st Marine Division, 7th Infantry Division and 3rd Infantry Division — in the Hamhung/Hungnam area. His goal was for the 50,000-plus troops to launch an offensive with the objective of reaching the Yalu as soon as possible. By the third week of November, the divisions were scattered across an area of several thousand square kilometers of rough mountainous terrain. It was one of the most forbidding landscapes in the world, the mountains rising to 8,000 feet with only footpaths and wagon trails available to cross them. At times, our troops had to blast through the narrow passageways to get their vehicles through.

The 1st Marine Division was more than 70 kilometers inland, attacking along both sides of the Chosin Reservoir, a long lake elevated upon a plateau north of the Hamhung/Hungnam area. At this time of year the reservoir was frozen solid though in warmer weather it flowed into a power plant several thousand feet below. The 7th Division was further east and one of its regiments, the 17th Infantry, advanced to the Yalu River on November 21. Other units of the division were separated by as much as 100 kilometers as General Almond relentlessly drove the forces north. Although the enemy offered light resistance against the advances of X Corps, the obstacles of terrain and brutally cold weather were daunting.

On the western flank, the Eighth Army continued sporadic attacks and, in turn, the Chinese intermittently struck back. It was evident that the Chinese were marshaling their forces for an all-out offensive. On the night of November 25th a force of 200,000 Chinese launched a formidable attack against the Eighth Army. Ringing bells, beating drums, blowing horns, and screaming blood-curdling yells, the boisterous Chinese rattled the nerves of our soldiers. This attack signaled the onset of one of the most intense and deadliest periods of the Korean War.

Though fighting valiantly, most ROK soldiers were captured, wounded or killed. The 2nd Infantry Division took up defensive positions along the Chongchon River. Among the division's regiments, the 9th Infantry suffered the most severe casualties. Its 38th Infantry, which I would later command, was practically wiped out at Kunu-Ri, a communication center situated along a north-south road. The 38th Infantry's casualties were so heavy that some spots in the roads were made impassable by dead bodies. Vehicles transporting the wounded were so full and cramped

Grieving the loss of a friend, August 28, 1950, Korea.
PHOTO BY AL CHANG, U.S. ARMY

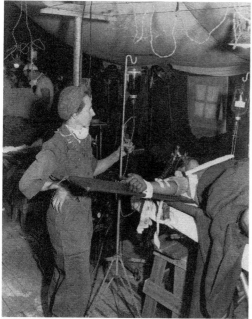

Above: American soldiers killed in action are loaded aboard the USS Randall, March 11, 1951.
PHOTO BY C.K. ROSE, U.S. NAVY

Left: Army nurse Capt. Sylvia Pavolvich, US Eighth Army, administers blood to wounded US X Corps soldier in Korea.
U.S. ARMY PHOTO

that some of the wounded beat off others attempting to board. The 23rd Infantry, in the meantime, was able to fight a rear-guard action and established a defensive position north of Pyongyang.

While IX Corps was experiencing heavy casualties due to enemy action, the X Corps had few casualties incurred by the enemy but many due to the severe weather. Cold weather gear had not yet been developed. Soldiers tried to keep warm by wearing multiple layers of clothing. I wore over-sized shoes in order to accommodate three pairs of socks, and donned three pairs of wool underwear and two overcoats. Most of us also stuffed one sleeping bag into another for extra warmth. Space heaters were few and far between and those available were placed in caves where troops could huddle in 15-minute intervals to thaw out before being sent back to the perimeter. Nothing appeared capable of fending off the exposure to such extreme temperatures. We even tried a few Eskimo techniques, like rubdowns with lard, but that proved ineffective. Many soldiers had their limbs amputated due to gangrene.

As we grappled with these sub-zero temperatures, the Chinese simultaneously attacked the Eighth Army in the west and the X Corps in the east. The 1st Marine Division advanced slowly, careful to keep its line of supply open. This helped them keep their units intact to fend off Chinese attacks. Struck in force, the Marines fought a successful rear-guard action south to the Chosin Reservoir, where they established a defensive perimeter. In contrast because the 7th Division was spread out, when it was struck by superior forces, its rear guard action was unsuccessful.

My challenge was how to keep our equipment running in the extreme cold temperatures of 20 to 30 F below zero. We erected large warming tents at each end of the field into which we placed space heaters so that as the bulldozers smoothed the airstrip, the operators and machinery could warm up between passes. To loosen up the frozen earth, we set off explosive charges. It was a good idea in theory but not in practice. The warm dozer blades thawed the earth, causing it to stick to them. To solve the problem, I applied various lubricants to the blades, but only ski wax worked. Accordingly, I requested that 200 pounds of ski wax be airlifted from Japan. Some wag at *Stars and Stripes*, the U.S. military newspaper, got wind of this and printed an article castigating me for the air delivery. It said I preferred skiing to conducting a war and was wasting taxpayer's money. In fact, what I was doing was trying to save lives.

Our warming tents soon came under fire from the Chinese, who intermittently closed in on our perimeter, lobbed in mortar shells and then disappeared. By the time a patrol would locate the base from which the mortar shells were fired, the Chinese moved on to set up another base elsewhere.

Army Corps of Engineers, Korea, 1950.
ROWNY PHOTO COLLECTION

During all of this, we still had to contend with the cold. The winters in North Korea were quite dry with very little snow but when the wind whipped up, which it did sporadically, the temperature dropped another 10 degrees and a light powdery snow formed clouds resembling massive dust storms. When that happened, we could not see more than a few feet ahead, but we still pressed on with our efforts to construct a usable airfield. After a great deal of hard work, we finally succeeded. With the help of some courageous pilots who navigated their planes despite the treacherous visibility and rough landing surface, we airlifted hundreds of casualties in valiant efforts to leave no wounded behind. This effort was augmented by over 1,500 tons of critically needed supplies dropped into the perimeter by parachute between 29 November and 9 December.

While the airstrip was being constructed, Major General O.P. Smith, the commander of the 1st Marine Division, who had been a stickler for doctrine during the Inchon invasion, did a good job organizing an effective defensive perimeter. The perimeter was in the form of a circle about 1½-miles in diameter. Colonel Chesty Puller, the regimental commander who performed so brilliantly pushing north after the invasion, walked the perimeter to raise the marines' morale. He boldly risked his life to enemy fire by going from position to position, navigating the five-mile circumference to give pep talks to the defending marines, convincing them that they were pinning down five attacking Chinese divisions. Colonel Ray Murray, another regimental commander, surely would have been right alongside Puller but was on crutches from the wound he incurred at Inchon. The third regimental commander, Colonel Wilburt "Big Foot" Brown, proved to be an intrepid leader, cut from the same cloth as Puller and Murray.

With the airstrip completed, I set my sights on how to span the Koto-Ri chasm, a precipitous cleft in the earth, which varied from 30 to 100 feet in width. I put the question to my engineer staff back in Hungnam. Major Al Wilder, who had been my battalion executive in World War II, suggested using a C-119 cargo plane to airdrop parts of a treadway bridge near the chasm's edge and then bolt the sections together.

It was an ambitious idea whose biggest obstacle was finding an Air Force pilot brave enough to airdrop the sections since most argued that it couldn't be done. They said it would be impossible to keep the aircraft under control because the airplane's weight would shift too dramatically when parts were unloaded.

Fortunately, we found one pilot who disagreed. To test the concept, we had him drop some treadway segments into friendly territory, south of Hungnam. With great skill, he was able to keep the aircraft stable, although the bridge parts fared less well. The parachutes intended to float the parts to earth didn't open properly and they plummeted down and wound up in a huge pile of twisted steel. With additional parachutes and careful rigging, we corrected the problem. The next day, to huge sighs of relief, we dropped the bridge parts into the southern portion of the perimeter. This was made possible by the highly skilled parachute riggers of the 8081st Quartermaster Company and the courageous C-119 pilots of 1503rd Air Transport Wing, both located in Japan. To quote from the company's archives, "When it comes to handing out plaudits to the Army, the Marines generally change the conversation to the Halls of Montezuma or talk about the weather. But if the talk gets around to the day the Army's paratrooper Quartermasters airmailed them a bridge, the song is a lot sweeter."

Engineers immediately scrambled to assemble the bridge at the chasm's narrowest point. Assembling the bridge would take about two hours. To afford the engineers those critical hours, the Marines, led by Army artillery officer Lieutenant Colonel John U.D. Page, held off the enemy. Page gained time by skillfully outflanking the enemy. Due to these efforts, the firing upon our bridge builders all but ceased, allowing the bridge to be assembled.

When the bridge was ready, the engineers pushed it over a fulcrum to span the chasm. It was perhaps one of the most amazing feats of bridge engineering on record. With the bridge in place, the Marines quickly exited the perimeter in an orderly fashion while fighting off the pursuing enemy. After crossing the chasm, they sent out patrols to the right and

Left: Supplies descend to U.S. and allied troops in Korea.
U.S. AIR FORCE PHOTO

Below: The only way out for U.S. forces withdrawing from the Chosin Reservoir. Air Force C-119s dropped portable bridge sections to span the chasm, allowing men and equipment to reach safety.
U.S. AIR FORCE PHOTO

left to protect their flanks. It couldn't have been a more professionally executed military operation. This enabled us to transport the wounded and the dead, who would not be abandoned to the frozen wasteland.

Lieutenant Colonel Page continued his heroics to make this happen. At one point, he plunged into the heart of a hostile position, so surprising the enemy that its ranks suffered heavy casualties as Page single-handedly engaged them until he was mortally wounded. He was posthumously awarded the Medal of Honor.

Experiencing moderate casualties, the Marines and the remaining elements of the 7th Division assembled at the port of Hungnam. General Almond ordered the 3rd Division to establish a defensive perimeter so the remainder of X Corps could evacuate in an orderly fashion. I was put in charge of that evacuation, which proceeded smoothly with the 3rd Division fending off sporadic Chinese hit-and-run attacks.

Destruction of Hungnam Harbor, Korea.
ROWNY PHOTO COLLECTION

46

After the 3rd Division that had been holding the perimeter was evacuated, I stayed back to oversee the demolition of the port. We were ordered to destroy whatever supplies we could not take with us; nothing of value was to be left for the Chinese. Having evacuated all of the troops and most of the supplies, we placed dozens of dynamite charges along the strategic piers of Hungnam. As the charges were detonated, the port went up in bright flashes of light and intense smoke.

Meanwhile on the west of the Korean peninsula, shortly after the Chinese began their massive attack, General Walker fought a rear-guard action back to the 38th parallel. This was ably executed, due in large part to the courageous performance of the Turkish Brigade, a part of the U.N. coalition. However, tragedy struck two days prior to Christmas. General Walker was inspecting troops north of Seoul when his driver attempted to pass a northbound convoy and was blindsided by an ROK truck that pulled out from a side road. The driver could not turn quickly enough and the jeep crashed, killing Walker.

US Officers and Edward L. Rowny watching the destruction of the harbor at Hungnam, Korea.
ROWNY PHOTO COLLECTION

On the east coast, while we were still evacuating supplies, Marine Colonel Fourney came to me with an urgent plea. He wanted to evacuate 100,000 North Koreans as a humanitarian move. The original idea came from U.S. educated Korean doctor, Hyun, Bong Hak. I knew Fourney quite well and in fact, Almond's second in command, General Ruffner, was always mixing the two of us up. I always came out on top. When Fourney did well, Ruffner congratulated me; if I screwed up, Fourney was balled-out. I felt I owed him one since I had been credited with his successes. For days, North Koreans had been queuing up in sub-zero temperatures, hoping there might be a place for them on an outbound ship to escape the certain death they faced from the advancing communists. We took the matter to General Almond who agreed.

On Christmas Eve 1950, in what became known as "Operation Christmas Cargo," we tucked North Koreans into the nooks and crannies of our ships — literally into every corner where we could find space. In the end we were only able to take 98,000. While travelling south on the 36-hour journey to Pusan two died but two more were born on the way.

I had supervised the transport of all supplies that could be fit into the cargo ships. About a dozen small boats, each piloted by two soldiers, carried the last of the supplies to our command ship, the Mount McKinley.

I, along with my radioman and jeep driver looked forward to boarding the last of the boats. To our horror it exploded before our eyes about a hundred yards from shore. My best guess is that one of the pilots, perhaps grabbing his last puff of a cigarette, threw down a butt, igniting some discarded gunpowder. The boat sank in a matter of minutes, sending its pilots to a watery grave. Our hearts sank as we watched the Mount McKinley, our ride home, sail off into the horizon.

North Korean refugees walk to the south.
PHOTO BY WALTER CALMUS, U.S. ARMY

My two colleagues and I were abandoned ashore. They were armed with carbines; I had only a pistol. We wondered how long it would be before I had to take off my white shirt and signal surrender to the Chinese who were closing in. My radioman tried to call for help but the radio was dead.

Fortunately, we spotted a U.S. plane passing overhead. My clever jeep driver spotted several casts of abandoned powered milk. He suggested that we spell out SOS-USA in large letters on the black asphalt of the nearby airfield. Seeing our signal, the pilot bravely came in to rescue us.

Evacuation of North Korean refugees by Americans.
U.S. NAVY PHOTO

The advancing Chinese fired on the plane while we boarded, but fortunately did not hit us. Admiral Doyle, the captain of the ship that I was supposed to have boarded, later told me that he thought we all had gone down with the boat that sank, which is why he sailed off. But I was very much alive.

Two hours later, I landed at Tachikawa Air Base near Tokyo. Soon after, having arrived at my family quarters in Tokyo, I surprised my astonished wife. My children took it in stride saying that Santa Claus arrived early. We had my radio operator and driver join us for a delicious turkey dinner. The next morning, as though nothing was out of the ordinary, we opened Christmas presents.

By midday, I received a message from General Almond who had been told by the pilot at Tachikawa that I was alive and in Tokyo. In characteristic terse language his message read: "I'm glad you made it. Be back at X Corps headquarters on December 27."

So much for my grand resurrection from the dead. Two days later, I caught a plane at Tachikawa and arrived back at X Corps headquarters on time.

I was greeted by General Ruffner, the chief of staff, who said, "Fourney, I am glad you are alive. Welcome back."

NATIONAL ARCHIVES AND RECORDS ADMINISTRATION PHOTO

I told him I continued to be puzzled by the way he confused me with Colonel Fourney.

SS Meredith Victory transports North Korean refugees, December 1950.
U.S. NAVY PHOTO

Ruffner looked at me with a twinkle in his eye and quite characteristically said, "Fourney, you did a good job."

During the three months between the liberation of Seoul and our evacuation from Hungnam, I corresponded with General Wood whenever possible. He wrote he had found his niche as a town planner, and received more requests for his services than he could accept. He had moved from the nuts and bolts of town planning to serving as a consultant. This, he said, allowed him to be an architect rather than a builder; it gave him the opportunity to dream rather than toil away. It was also more lucrative and provided him with funds to send talented young men and women to college.

Wood's fascination with events in Korea was unwavering. He expressed disappointment that General Abe Lincoln allowed his ego to influence his choice of the 38th parallel. We agreed his was Lincoln's only departure from selflessness and recommending the best military course of action. I said I too felt let down by my mentor but excused him on the grounds that he knew the Soviets would not have agreed to the 39th parallel since it would have allowed U.N. forces to be within artillery range of the North Korean capital. He swore that he could have predicted some of the difficulties we encountered and believed many could have been avoided had Almond's X Corps been assigned to Walker's Eighth Army. He insisted that it was a mistake for General MacArthur to allow Almond to report directly to him at the top, as it was bound to cause personality clashes between Almond and Walker. I disagreed. If Almond's X Corps had been made part of Walker's Eighth Army, Almond's aggressiveness would have been lost. Moreover, MacArthur had lost his confidence in Walker.

Most of our correspondence was devoted to the political situation following the liberation of Seoul. General Wood wrote that it was a responsibility of the president to issue clear-cut military instructions to his subordinates. I agreed, saying that this would have avoided the confusion of differing messages from the Joint Chiefs of Staff and the newly appointed secretary of defense. However, President Truman was caught in an awkward position. The CIA apparently did not know whether the Chinese would enter into Korea following the liberation of Seoul. We discussed the possibility that President Truman elected not to clear up the contradictory orders coming from the Pentagon. Politically, he wanted to recapture North Korea, but he also did not want to provoke the Chinese into moving south into the ROK. Thus there may have been political reasons for the ambiguity.

Wood said the president could have clarified the situation when he met with MacArthur at Wake Island. But the president was weeks away from an election and the U.S. public was basking in MacArthur's success at Inchon. The general's enormous prestige allowed him to do what he wanted. It is not hard to guess what might have happened if MacArthur had followed the Joint Chiefs' instructions and permitted only ROK forces beyond the "neck" of the peninsula at Pyongyang. When U.N. forces went north towards the Yalu, the ROK forces were practically obliterated by the Chinese. The Chinese had actually made their decision to intervene when U.N. forces crossed the 38th parallel.

General Wood believed, in the absence of clear instructions, MacArthur was correct in using all of his forces to attempt to liberate North Korea. He believed that when the Chinese destroyed two-thirds of the 7th Cavalry, MacArthur should have moved to establish a defensive position along the 38th parallel. Still, he wrote that MacArthur's fatal error was in being slow to realize that Chinese troops had, in fact, infiltrated North Korea. Wood blamed General

General Almond awarding the Legion of Merit to Edward L. Rowny.
ROWNY PHOTO COLLECTION

Willoughby, the Eighth Army intelligence chief, for not correctly assessing the Chinese situation. Ultimately, he blamed MacArthur because he was in command.

Wood gave me high marks for using ski wax when I built the airstrip within the Chosin perimeter. He said that airlifting the wounded to hospitals saved hundreds of lives. He praised me even more for air dropping sections of the bridge, which allowed the surrounded troops at the Chosin reservoir to return to safety. Wood characteristically took credit for these two engineering feats, saying it was his training program in the 41st Engineers that made them possible. The general appeared to be touched when we talked about the Christmas Cargo evacuation of 100,000 North Koreans.

The events between the capture of Seoul and evacuation from Hungnam continued to be topics of conversation between Wood and me for years.

19 | Moral Dilemmas & Moral Courage in Korea

Arriving back in Korea, I was shocked that General Almond appointed me chief of logistics of X Corps. I was succeeding Colonel Aubrey Smith, a brilliant officer who was murdered while on leave in Tokyo. His wife stabbed him after finding him in bed with the Japanese maid. I told General Almond I preferred to stay in operations since that was my background. With a grin, he said, "You know me well enough to know that I'm my own operations officer." I'd seen that first-hand in Italy when Almond maneuvered battalions like pieces on a chessboard.

Almond anticipated that we would be fighting back up the peninsula and the need for fuel, food and ammunition would become our greatest problem. The general added, "Napoleon said that an Army marches on its stomach." Closer to home, Eisenhower said, "Wars are won or lost by logistics."

General Matthew Ridgway replaced General Walker, the commanding general of Eighth Army who was killed in a jeep accident on December 23. Ridgway's combat record in WWII was brilliant. He commanded airborne operations behind the German defenses during the landings in Normandy. He also led similar operations that helped Patton advance. He was known as "Old Iron Tits" for wearing two grenades at chest level.

General Ridgway's first task was to determine whether the Eighth Army had the strength to advance north or whether it should evacuate to Japan. Potentially, the enemy had an almost infinite supply of troops with which to attack, but we didn't know whether they would use them. Was it wiser to stay or call it quits? What would be the value of staying if we could not move north?

Ridgway assembled the commanders of I, IX, and X Corps and their staffs in a schoolhouse auditorium. He and the three corps commanders were on the stage and we staffers were the audience.

The commanders of I and IX Corps, each in his own style, delivered the same message. They told Ridgway the Eighth Army had been badly beaten up and was in no position to undertake offensive operations. Opposing their view, General Almond said that despite its defeats, the Eighth Army was battle-hardened and could fight its way back to the 38th parallel.

After hearing the arguments, General Ridgway took the three corps commanders to a room offstage to deliberate. When they returned, Ridgway stood center stage and grasped a grenade on his harness with his left hand and thrusting out his right hand pointed north.

"Gentlemen," he proclaimed, "we're going that way!"

The I and IX Corps staff members were stunned, believing their chiefs made the better arguments. One said, "Oh shit." Another muttered, "Wrong way Ridgway." We in the X Corps staff stood and applauded. General Almond was elated. His wish came true: the Eighth Army would stay in Korea and take on the Communists.

Preparing to launch an offensive, we were surprised when the enemy attacked our perimeter in force on New Year's Eve 1950. Aided by heavy artillery bombardment and close air support from Japan, we halted their advance. Confident that we had the superior force, Ridgway again prepared to take the offensive. In the first week of February, the Eighth Army, with X Corps in the lead, succeeded in pushing back the enemy. Continuing their steady advance, by mid-February, we captured the major city of Suwon, 20 miles south of Seoul.

General Matthew Ridgway
U.S. ARMY

Bringing down reinforcements from the north, the enemy launched a counteroffensive. This attack was stopped due largely to the bravery of the 23rd Infantry Regiment, one of three regiments of the 2nd Infantry Division. Much of the success of the 23rd Infantry could be attributed to its attached French battalion. This battalion consisted of volunteers who had fought in WWII against the Nazis. It was a courageous unit commanded by a three-star general, Ralph Monclar, who took a voluntary reduction to lieutenant colonel to take command. Although the 23rd Infantry was successful, it incurred a large number of casualties.

By this point, General Ridgway had revived the morale of the stricken Eighth Army by relying heavily on the aggressiveness of General Almond and X Corps. Toward the end of the month, the revitalized Eighth Army began a series of counterattacks resulting in the recapture of Seoul on March 14.

Meanwhile, with the help of thousands of KATUSAs, Korean civilians pressed into service, we rebuilt roads, bridges, railroad tracks and constructed airfields for our moves north. The railroads were particularly important since Korean roads were poor and impassable. Over a thousand miles of tracks needed rebuilding, a job that included replacing all the ties the enemy had stolen for firewood.

South Korean laborers and US soldiers carry ammunition and food up a mountainside to troops of the 8th Cavalry Regiment, 1st Cavalry Division (Infantry), engaged in action against the Communist led North Korean forces in the Waegwan area.
U.S. ARMY PHOTO

I brought locomotives and boxcars in from Japan and put the rail line back into service. I also built runways in the southern part of Korea so that urgently needed supplies could be delivered by air. The request for supplies, like fuel and ammunition, had become so great that the Air Force was delivering 200 tons a day to airstrips in Korea.

In March and April, attacks and counterattacks seesawed along the 38th parallel, and Seoul was lost and recaptured several times. The enemy possessed larger numbers of soldiers than the Eighth Army, but their lack of air power and artillery support inhibited their effectiveness. During the fighting, their troops usually suffered four to five times our number of casualties. They were able to make limited advances using massive attacks, but were generally beaten back by the better-supported and heroic Eighth Army.

As early as the spring of 1951, General MacArthur apparently wanted to expand the conflict to an all-out war against China. This, however, risked war with the Soviets and jeopardized the stability of Europe. MacArthur thought the war against communism could only be won by attacking China. President Truman disagreed. His top priority was countering the threat of the Soviet Union in Europe. He was content to allow Korea to remain divided along the 38th parallel. In this he had the full backing of his secretaries of state and defense and the Joint Chiefs.

On April 11, 1951, one of our radio operators alerted us to listen to an important announcement. We were stunned at what we heard. General MacArthur had been relieved of his command. He was highly respected by the military, and most senior officers of the Eighth Army were shocked and deeply saddened. General Almond was crestfallen.

Busy fighting the war, we were unaware that in Washington, tensions between General MacArthur and the president had reached a breaking point. Congressman Joseph Martin, Jr., the minority leader of the House of Representatives, made an inflammatory speech on the House floor. He said that the president was denying MacArthur the means to achieve victory. Martin read a letter from MacArthur agreeing with him, which concluded with the words, "We must win. There is no substitute for victory." This did not sit well with the president, who had just made it clear he was prepared to settle for a deadlock in Korea.

We did not know at that time that MacArthur had repeatedly sought permission to make air attacks north of the Yalu and even

Left to right: General Douglas MacArthur, Ambassador to Korea John Muccio, President Harry Truman, October 14, 1950.
DEPT. OF STATE PHOTO

considered laying a defensive band of radiation, from detonated nuclear weapons, along the border. He also pushed to have Chinese Nationalists in Formosa — who had been run off the mainland by Communist forces — brought into the Korean War. MacArthur truly was willing to risk all for success.

Reading accounts of what transpired in Washington, it was clear that there was more behind President Truman's decision to relieve General MacArthur than the speech by Representative Martin. It roused the ire of the Republican congressman, who called for the president's impeachment. In his cabinet meetings, both Secretaries Acheson and Marshall agreed that the president had no other option than to fire MacArthur.

General Ridgway was appointed to succeed MacArthur as commander in chief of U.N. forces. General James Van Fleet, a highly decorated WWII hero, replaced Ridgway. Ridgway's first instructions to his successor were to vigorously defend the Eighth Army's front-line position, and while truce talks had begun in March, he wanted Van Fleet to keep fighting to increase negotiating leverage for the peace talks, which were in their early stages.

On May 19, Ridgway flew from his Tokyo headquarters to Korea to meet with his corps commanders and lay out plans for a new offensive north of the 38th parallel. IX Corps was ordered to seize the high ground near the Chongchon basin, in the middle of the peninsula, the southernmost part of the "Iron Triangle." The X Corps attacked to the right of the IX Corps, and the I Corps to their left.

With good weather and heavy air support, the Eighth Army quickly advanced to the north, reaching the 39th parallel. By the end of May, however, heavy rains made further advances impossible. Ridgway ordered General Van Fleet to dig in and reinforce the defensive positions along what was known as the Kansas Line. This line was a diagonal, which crossed the 38th parallel, south of the parallel on the west and north of it in the east. During the next several months while truce talks continued, there were numerous attacks and counterattacks along the Kansas Line.

Throughout this time I was kept busy providing logistical support for the X Corps. Muddy roads made moving supplies forward difficult. We relied mostly on "Chogi bearers," Korean laborers who carried about 70 pounds of supplies on wooden A-frames strapped to their backs. We built supply depots as we went forward, a few warehouses at a time. We were also still bringing in a sizable portion of our supplies from Japan by air, dropping much of it by parachute. This was a costly way to supply troops since high winds often scattered supplies. I built 15 airfields on our drive north since it was more efficient to deliver air supplies by cargo planes than parachuting them from the air.

My job was made more difficult because the Army doubled the daily allotment of artillery rounds. The infantry welcomed more fire support, but keeping ammunition moving forward was a formidable task.

In early June, General Almond told me that if I would volunteer to stay in Korea for a second year he would give me command of an infantry regiment. Most of his regimental commanders led regiments in WWII and he considered them too old to lead troops in the difficult Korean terrain. Almond knew that I had been promoted rapidly and was younger and more vigorous than most of his regimental commanders. He said he would make me the executive officer of the 38th "Rock of the Marne" Infantry, a regiment of the 2nd Infantry Division. If I performed satisfactorily, as he assumed I would, he would assign me the command of the infantry regiment. Colonel Frank Mildren, a fellow West Pointer from the class of 1939, commanded the reconstituted 38th. He performed with great valor in WWII, commanding the 1st Battalion of the 38th Infantry in the Battle of the Bulge, for which it won a presidential citation. This award for a unit was equivalent to the Distinguished Service Cross for individuals. The 38th Regiment Mildren now commanded was the successor to the unit in which he had commanded a battalion.

General Almond handpicked Mildren to serve in the X Corps. When the plan of the Inchon invasion was approved, General MacArthur told Washington he needed 25 of the best colonels in the Army to make the invasion succeed. He argued that since the invasion force was small and consisted of poorly trained troops, he needed to make up the deficit with superior leaders. Mildren was one of the 25 and General Almond made him his Plans and Operations officer (G-3). It was a pleasure to serve on the Corps staff with such a fine officer when I became the X Corps Engineer.

When Colonel Mildren took command of the 38th Infantry, he was faced with an enormous challenge. In November of the preceding year, five Chinese divisions descended upon the 2nd Infantry Division. The 38th Infantry took the brunt of that attack, and approximately 90 percent of its troops were killed or wounded. As a result, Colonel Mildren's reconstituted regiment consisted almost entirely of replacements from the U.S. The battle-hardened soldiers of the 38th who survived Kunu-Ri recounted their experiences to the new recruits, severely demoralizing them. Mildren called the Kunu-Ri veterans together and told them in no uncertain terms to save their "war stories" for after the war. Exhibiting superb leadership, he honed his regiment into an excellent fighting force.

Like most U.S. infantry regiments in Korea, the 38th consisted of four battalions: three organic battalions and a foreign contingent, in this case from the Netherlands. This configuration was similar to other regiments where the fourth battalion also consisted of troops from other countries with forces committed to the United Nations Command in Korea. The 23rd Infantry of the 2nd Division had the battalion from France mentioned above; the 9th Infantry Regiment had a battalion from Thailand. The Dutch soldiers were volunteers from 18 geographical areas around the world who had been given only basic training.

Although the Dutch battalion had not trained as a unit before it arrived in Korea, it soon became an efficient fighting force. When the enemy attacked U.N. forces in February 1951, their offensives included infiltrating the retreating ROK forces and striking the Dutch battalion. The spirited Dutch fought fiercely but suffered over 100 casualties including the loss of their commander, Lieutenant Colonel Den Ouden. In May, the Dutch unit was again attacked by a superior Chinese force, during which the new commanding officer and two company commanders were killed. The actions of the Dutch battalion were so valiant they were twice awarded the Presidential Unit Citation, more than any other unit in the Korean War.

In mid-July, General Almond left Korea and assumed command of the Army War College. It was not a great surprise; he had served in Korea since the Inchon invasion, longer than any other corps commander. Fortunately, I had worked for his successor, Lieutenant General Clovis Byers, and greatly admired him. He told me he would follow through with General Almond's promise to give me command of an infantry regiment.

At the end of July General Ridgway, believing he could shorten our defensive line ordered General Van Fleet to advance to the 39th parallel — the wasp waist. While the shorter defense line would require fewer troops, Van Fleet argued that it was not worth the losses we would incur to reach that position. Ridgway agreed and the attack was called off. For the next several months while truce talks continued, fighting was confined to improving defensive positions along the ridges of the Kansas line. The two most famous ones were known as Bloody Ridge and Heartbreak Ridge, the highest grounds in the area and parts of a Chinese-occupied series of connected hills, each several miles long.

As September approached, we were ordered to get more aggressive. Mildren said he needed to rest and would allow me to plan and execute a major battle. He said he would take full responsibility but allow me complete freedom. It was unusual for an executive officer to be given such responsibility and an exciting opportunity. I was also pleased because it would allow Mildren, who had been pushing himself extremely hard, to get some much-needed rest.

General Robert Young, commander of the 2nd Infantry Division, ordered Colonel Mildren to capture Hill 1243. He turned this assignment over to me. Hill 1243 was northwest of the Punch Bowl, a flat piece of terrain bordered by mountains on three sides. Taking it would replace the North Korean firepower with our own.

Capturing hill 1243 would not be easy. Our tanks could not climb its steep slopes, and there was no place to station artillery to support the attack. To provide a large amount of fire support, I decided to set up firebases on three lower hills nearby that could deliver 75-mm rockets and 4.5-inch mortar shells to the top of Hill 1243. I parked the tanks and artillery pieces at the bottom of the hill and, much to the disgust of the tank and artillery crews, put them to work on foot. Each tanker and artilleryman was placed in charge of 50 Chogi-bearers, who carried rockets and mortar shells to the firebases. It took these human supply trains about five hours to carry ammunition up to a firebase and about three to return.

After an eight-hour break to rest their tired and often bloody feet, the crews were given another load to take to the hilltop bases. We worked Chogi-bearers round the clock, and after three days and two nights, had amassed gigantic stockpiles of ammunition atop the hills.

The plan called for delivering an extraordinarily heavy barrage of fire — some six times greater than normal — on Hill 1243. Following the heavy barrage, the regiment, led by our bold Dutch battalion, would charge to the top of the hill. With the Dutch unit's thousand or so soldiers and our three U.S. battalions, the offensive would involve about 4,000 men. We estimated that the North Koreans holding the hill numbered between 1,000 and 2,000.

The offensive was to begin at dawn, September 3, 1951. But a heavy fog rolled in, forcing me to postpone our attack until 1000. General Young was not pleased. At 1000, the hill was still socked in and I postponed the charge yet another hour. At 1100, I was explaining the delay to General Young, who had called to ask if I had taken the hill.

"Damn it," he said. "I need that hill. The troops on the lower ridges are taking a beating. I want you bastards to take hill 1243 immediately."

Since the fog was still heavy, I postponed the attack once more — this time to noon. General Young was even more annoyed.

"Once again, I'm telling you that I want you bastards to take that hill," he said, "or I will relieve you."

Just before noon the fog finally lifted, and I ordered the firebases to begin their heavy barrage of mortar and rocket fire. This heavy bombardment lasted three times longer than usual. The hilltop was literally paved with steel. Our devastating barrage completely unnerved the North Koreans, who hunkered more deeply into their defensive positions. The Dutch forces "walked the artillery," moving forward in 50-meter increments, up to the edge of where each prior barrage had ended. When our troops were 100 meters from the top, I ordered a final 5 minutes of heavy firing from the three hilltops. I told Major Johan Christianson, the executive of the Dutch battalion who was personally leading the assault, to sprint for the top of the hill as soon as the barrage lifted.

To my horror, as I was watching the action from a light observation plane, I saw our leading Dutch element charging for the top of the hill even though the final barrage still had two minutes to go. I immediately ordered the firing to cease, but the order came too late. I saw a dozen Dutch soldiers fall to the ground but did not know if they fell from enemy or friendly fire. I suspected the latter. The Dutch soldiers charged right into our own maelstrom. They rapidly took the hill.

As soon as I realized the attack was a success, I had my pilot take me to the bottom of the hill, where I transferred to a helicopter that flew me to the top. There, I surveyed the vast damage we had inflicted on the North Koreans. Hundreds of North Koreans had been killed or wounded, but our casualties were light and we did not suffer a single fatality. In their haste to avoid the heavy bombardment, the retreating North Koreans uncharacteristically left some wounded behind. They later told us they were happy to be captured since our medical treatment was far superior to what they could expect. I complimented Major Christianson on a magnificent job. I apologized for the misunderstanding about the length of the final barrage, which resulted in several of his soldiers being hit.

"There was no misunderstanding," he said. "I deliberately ordered my men forward two minutes early. Our Dutch doctrine teaches that we are to hug our supporting fire closely. To us, this means that fires are not lifted until we experience the first casualty due to friendly fire. We have learned through experience that this results in fewer overall casualties."

Startled, I asked the major not to repeat that story to anyone, since I would be relieved if it became known that casualties had been deliberately caused by friendly fire.

I had arranged a surprise for the men for a job well done. I'd brought my chef along in the helicopter and, anticipating the successful offensive, had him bring along a home-style feast. Before long, the men were chowing down on Southern fried chicken, mashed potatoes and corn on the cob, washed down by beer and cokes. It was as though a bit of America's heartland had forged its way to the top of a former den of communism.

Soon afterwards, General Young landed by helicopter on top of the hill. Pleased at our light casualties and the feast the soldiers were enjoying, he congratulated us for a job well done.

"You are a bunch of wonderful bastards," he said. "With the capture of Hill 1243, our units on the ridges below will have an easier job accomplishing their mission."

That wrapped up an extraordinarily successful operation that I consider the high point of my military career. Although close to 200 North Koreans were killed and three times as many wounded, we suffered perhaps two-dozen wounded but not a single fatality.

After capturing Hill 1243, I resumed my job as the executive officer of the regiment. Colonel Mildren once again relied on me, for the most part, to provide the regiment logistical support, while he devoted his energies to commanding the regiment. My logistics work was often mundane and boring but providing ammunition, gasoline and food at the regimental level was just as critical as it had been earlier, when I was a logistics chief of the Corps. Logistics in

Korea often took priority over tactics since the availability of supplies — and our ability to transport them over rugged terrain — determined what could and what could not be done.

In mid-October, Colonel Mildren gave me another opportunity to command an operation. Intelligence reports indicated that the Chinese occupied a hill some three miles to the rear of their front line and were apparently fortifying it against our possible advance. I discussed with Mildren the great potential helicopters had for vertical envelopments. Fortunately, the marine regiment adjacent to ours had ten helicopters used primarily for supply purposes. I convinced the marine commander to let me borrow his helicopters for a raid against the dug-in Chinese we called the "Black Diamond Gang." The aggressive commander, like most marines, always looking for a fight, readily agreed.

I asked my battalion commanders to each recruit 100 volunteers. More than that stepped forward, and we selected the 100 best suited for the mission. I assigned 10 soldiers to each of the 10 helicopters, stationing a soldier with a machine gun in the open door on one side of the helicopter and one with a 75-mm rocket launcher on the other side. I also furnished them with a large number of hand grenades. The plan was to have the helicopters fly just above the treetops until they were immediately over the enemy's position. The plan was that by flying the nap of the earth, the helicopters would be so low as to be undetected until they reached the objective. The helicopters would lay down a heavy barrage of fire and quickly land the troops before the shocked enemy had the chance to react.

The operation went off according to plan. The short but heavy barrage, together with fires from the landed troops, quickly killed, wounded or dispersed the Black Diamond Gang. None of our

1st Marine
Division captures
Chinese
Communists
on the central
Korean front,
March 2, 1951.
PHOTO BY PFC. C. T. WEHNER
(USMC)

soldiers were wounded nor were any of the helicopters seriously damaged. The operation was highly successful, and I looked forward to conducting similar operations once I got to command the regiment. However, serious negotiations with the North began soon afterward and offensive actions ceased.

At this point, the division chief of staff was wounded visiting the front. General Young designated me to take over until a replacement arrived from the States. It was an interesting job and allowed me to see the big picture of how all units of the division were integrated. The job also gave me the opportunity to get to know General Robert Young and his assistant division commander, Brigadier General Hayden Boatner. The familiarity proved invaluable since I would serve under each later.

On December 1, 1951, Colonel Mildren rotated to the U.S., and I assumed command of the 38th Infantry. Talks began in earnest at Panmunjon, just north of the border between North and South Korea. We were now in a "no war, no peace" situation. At the same time, we were under instructions from Washington to remain on high alert but not to undertake any major offensives. Instead, we were to patrol aggressively and capture prisoners. General Young insisted that we capture prisoners to learn the enemy's plans and where and when they might attack. The pressure to take prisoners was intense. Yet we had strict orders not to commit units larger than a platoon in size.

During the early weeks of the New Year, I repeatedly tried to capture prisoners. The usual tactic was to make surprise attacks at small outposts occupied by no more than a squad of enemy troops, but the raids proved nearly impossible to pull off. The Chinese were dug in and well protected in bunkers connected by underground tunnels, outposts that were further supported by artillery and mortar fire.

Nevertheless, General Young kept insisting that we capture prisoners. In early March, our intelligence sources reported a new enemy outpost on a hilltop 100 yards forward of their front-line positions. I aimed for it, committing a platoon of infantry supported by mortar and artillery fires. The day of the attack was extremely cold and soon after launching our charge, my men were pinned down by a heavy barrage of artillery. When I went to survey the situation, I learned that the platoon leader had decided against moving forward or back, fearing either would result in increased casualties. Instead, the troops just lay there in the extreme cold, relying on what little cover the terrain provided. They were frozen in position.

Not wanting to lose the entire platoon to the weather and enemy fire, I opted to use more force and committed the remainder of the company. I instructed the company commander to advance through the pinned-down platoon to accomplish the mission. In that way, there would be a renewed attempt to capture prisoners, but more importantly, our pinned down platoon would get out alive.

The tactic worked. Though several of our troops were wounded, there were no fatalities, and our troops snatched two wounded prisoners.

The next day General Boatner, then acting division commander, came to me with orders from Washington that stunned me. I was ordered to be relieved since I had violated instructions by committing more than a platoon to offensive action. I explained to General Boatner that I felt I had no choice; I risked losing the lives of an entire platoon if I didn't send in more troops. General Boatner was convinced that I had done the proper thing. He reported to Washington that he had investigated the situation and absolved me of any wrongdoing.

The next day General Boatner received a message that read: "Obey instructions. Relieve Rowny for having violated the order of not committing more than a platoon to action."

General Boatner wired back: "If you feel you must relieve someone, relieve me. I'm in command here."

I remained in charge of the regiment and heard nothing more of the incident. Apparently, Washington knew Boatner was not bluffing. To put it mildly, I was elated. It was a lesson in moral courage.

The next several months were uneventful. There were no offensive actions on either side as talks continued at Panmunjon. We were still pressed to capture prisoners, but after the incident in early March, the pressure lessened. In the meantime, I requested to be transferred from the Corps of Engineers to the Infantry, having commanded both an infantry battalion and regiment in combat. I figured there were eight four-star generals in the infantry while the chief of engineers, the top job in the corps, called for only three stars. My chances for promotion to general officer rank seemed much more promising in the infantry. Certainly Major Christianson was proof of that on the Dutch side.

North Korean and Chinese POWs in Pusan, Korea, April, 1951.
PHOTO BY LARRY GAHN, U.S. STATE DEPARTMENT

The brave infantry commander was promoted to Lieutenant Colonel during our time in Korea and much later, rose to become head of the Armed Forces of the Netherlands.

While waiting on my transfer request, the Army, anxious to give as many field-grade officers as possible the opportunity to command, ordered me to turn over my regiment. I was sent to Tokyo on temporary duty in the operations section of FECOM until the Army decided on my transfer. The request was finally approved and in July, I packed up my family and returned to San Francisco via a troop transport. There I picked up a new Ford station wagon and with my family drove across the country to Fort Benning, where I would start my new job as chief of the regimental tactics department.

During my time in Korea, I continued to correspond with General Wood. He said it was a good thing that X Corps, after being evacuated from Hungnam, was placed under Eighth Army command. This action removed General Almond's second hat as chief of staff and finally straightened out the command structure. He praised General Almond for helping convince General Ridgway that the Eighth Army should stay in Korea and attack to the north.

Wood agreed with Almond that there were times when logistics were more important than operations and he thought Almond's decision to put me in charge of logistics of the corps was a wise one. Napoleon had said that an army marches on its stomach, but we both concurred that in Korea, the Army marched forward against superior numbers through its massive artillery support. Wood was pleased as well that General Almond gave me the command of an infantry regiment. He said he was partially responsible for that since early-on, he had trained the 41st Engineers to fight as infantry.

As for General MacArthur, Wood felt that President Truman was entirely correct in relieving him. He added that MacArthur had acted unwisely, but his great contribution as a soldier entitled him to better treatment. Truman, he said, acted less than presidential when he publicly gloated over General MacArthur's downfall.

Wood told me my planning and execution of the battle of Hill 1243 was brilliant, and said its resounding success should have earned me a promotion to full colonel. It was ironic, he added, that the commanders of the battles of Heartbreak and Bloody Ridge received so much publicity and praise while I, who commanded the critical battle that saved them, went unnoticed. Still, I got the opportunity to experiment with helicopters in combat, and on that point, Wood was excited. He urged me to continue to develop the concept of sky cavalry.

General Wood was thrilled with my decision to transfer to the infantry and my assignment to the Infantry School. As always, he flattered and fanned my ego, insisting that I was on my way to four-star rank and to becoming chief of staff of the Army. He was looking forward to talking with me at great length upon my return to the U.S.

Epilogue

True to his word, in July 1970 General Westmoreland promoted me and assigned me to command the I Corps in Korea. The corps consisted of six Korean (ROK) divisions and two U.S. Army divisions. My job was to provide the left half of the defensive front from the west coast to the mountains in central Korea. The eastern half of the defensive line was manned by the ROK Army. Whereas the ROK troops were an ineffective force during the Korean War, they were now a well led, disciplined and highly trained fighting machine. My two U.S. Army Divisions, the Second and Seventh, were also first class, displaying none of the weaknesses of our troops in Vietnam.

The Army's decision to integrate the United States and ROK units into a single U.S.-ROK command made my time in Korea intriguing. Major General Jae Jon Lee, a capable Korean officer who spoke English fluently, was assigned as my deputy. He was invaluable to the formation of I Corps(ROK/US) Group. Although I in-

The Shield of Seoul I Corps (ROK/US) Group patch designed by General Edward L. Rowny, Commander, I Corp (ROK/US) Group with the help of Major General Lee Jae Jon, Deputy Commander, Korea, 1970. The group's motto was "Friendship Forged in Blood." ROWNY COLLECTION

sisted to the Department of Defense that the Koreans of my headquarters should live and eat together with us, I was told that the United States would not foot the bill. General Lee convinced the Korean Defense Minister to pay the difference between the Korean allowances and what they would need to live on the same scale with the American elements of my headquarters. This allowed us to operate together in a single integrated headquarters rather than in two separate parts.

The Korean Minster of Defense assigned to the Corps exceptional Korean officers who spoke English to make up the other half of my staff. I Corps(ROK/US) Group, after consolidation, consisted of seven ROK divisions and only a single U.S. division. I left Korea after a year confident that I Corps(ROK/US) Group could defeat any future attack by the North Koreans.

The epilogue is followed by two one-page excerpts, one from Chapter 22 and the second from Chapter 25.

Excerpts from
Chapters 22 *and* 25 *of*
Smokey Joe and the General

In our final analysis of General Marshal, General Wood and I agreed that seldom in U.S. history has one man been called upon to do so much for his country and do it so selflessly. Yet, we were uneasy about his conduct concerning the "bring the boys home" decision. Marshall had taught that if an officer disagreed with orders, he should respectfully and privately ask his commander to reconsider. If he failed, but believed that carrying out the orders would jeopardize national security, the honorable thing to do was resign. Only after leaving the service was an officer free to go public with his disagreement. President Truman's respect for Marshall was so high and his prestige so great that had Marshall threatened to resign when pressured to bring

General George C. Marshall, 1946.
OFFICIAL PHOTO

the boys home, we believed Truman might have reconsidered. Had the U.S. not demobilized so quickly and completely, the Korean War might have been avoided, the expansion of communism halted, and the Cold War averted. In view of the high stakes, General Wood and I painfully decided to deduct Marshall one point and gave him a score of 8 out of 9. We found it hard to criticize a man of such high virtue but philosophized that no man is perfect. Alas, even General Marshall had feet of clay.

Evaluating General MacArthur's character, Wood concluded that when it came to selflessness, MacArthur had none, and when it came to self-promotion, he had plenty. We agreed to deduct one point from his score for this shortcoming, and for the lack of integrity he displayed in falsifying his reports. We deducted a second point for his poor judgment in acting on questionable advice regarding the presence of Chinese troops in Korea and the letter criticizing Truman's conduct of the war. Weighing all the factors carefully, Wood and I awarded MacArthur a final score of 7 out of 9.

General Dwight D. Eisenhower, February 1, 1945.
U.S. ARMY PHOTO

Analyzing Eisenhower's career, General Wood and I agreed that his occasional lapses in duty and lack of selflessness necessitated the deduction of a full point from his score. We also concurred that another point should be deducted for his lack of judgment and disloyalty in failing to defend General Marshall against McCarthy's attacks. We gave him a final score of seven out of nine, putting him in a tie with General MacArthur.

Below is an edited version of parts of Chapter 25 of Smokey Joe and the General.

Secretary Vance said he was quite impressed with the Howze Board tests. He told me he was thinking of sending armed helicopters to Vietnam and testing them in a combat role.

Vance asked me who I thought should be put in charge of the tests he had in mind. I offered him the name of one I thought particularly qualified.

The next day, Vance told me the general I recommended declined the job because of his wife's illness. After talking with the chief of staff of the Army, Vance said he decided I was the one who should go to Vietnam.

It soon became clear that I would receive less than enthusiastic support in the Pentagon. General Earle "Bus" Wheeler, the Army's chief of staff, wanting to avoid confrontations with the other service chiefs, did not publicly endorse sending armed helicopters to Vietnam, even though he believed Army Aviation should be expanded. As newly appointed chairman, Taylor was not inclined to enter into a roles-and-missions fight early in his tenure. As a result, my orders from the secretary of the Army to proceed to Vietnam were not sanctioned by either Wheeler or Taylor.

During the stopover in Hawaii on my way to Vietnam, I paid a courtesy call on Admiral Harry Felt, commander in chief of Pacific Command (CINCPAC). He told me straight away something I already knew too well — that if the Army armed helicopters, it would violate approved roles and missions. Felt, who reported directly to the chairman of the Joint Chiefs, commanded all U.S. forces in Vietnam. He said he would not allow me to proceed because my instructions were issued by the secretary of the Army and not by his superior, the chairman of the Joint Chiefs.

While the admiral barred me from communicating in any way with the Army secretary, his communications chief did not see anything wrong with sending my message requesting a leave of absence for a vacation. In that way, without Felt's knowledge, I boarded a plane for Manila.

The chiefs were opposed to ACTIV operating in Vietnam for different reasons. The chief of staff of the Air Force was flatly opposed, insisting that arming Army helicopters was in violation of established roles and missions. The chief of naval operations feared armed Army helicopters would place the mission of naval strike aviation in jeopardy. The Army chief of staff, General Wheeler, was opposed on two counts. The first, as I knew full well, was that his staff was controlled by armor officers who believed that, within a fixed budget, each added helicopter in the Army's inventory meant one less tank. Second, he was aiming to become Joint Chiefs chairman and wanted to demonstrate broadmindedness by agreeing with the Air Force and Navy. To make matters worse, Chairman Taylor was reluctant to order his chiefs into line because they operated under a consensus rule.

General Edward L. Rowny experimenting with armed helicopters.
ROWNY PHOTO COLLECTION

Marines march North Korean prisoners across a rice paddy, 1950.
U.S. MARINES PHOTO

1st Cavalry Division Temporary Cemetery,
Taegu, Korea, August 25, 1950.
U.S. ARMY PHOTO

Soldiers under a bridge under construction
somewhere in Korea.
U.S. ARMY PHOTO

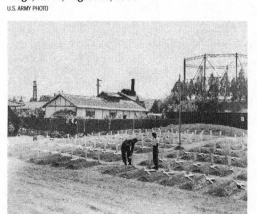

A close vigil is kept on Chinese Communists by PFC William Stinnett Jr. in Korea.
U.S. ARMY PHOTO

Wounded soldier gets needed help at mealtime.
U.S. ARMY PHOTO

Cpl. Elmer Soprano repairing communication lines from Tanyang to Chechon, Korea.
U.S. ARMY PHOTO

Medics prepare injured soldier for transport.
U.S. ARMY PHOTO

North Korean positions along the Naktong River are assaulted by 7th Cavalry Regiment.
U.S. ARMY PHOTO

Marines fighting in the streets of Seoul, September 1950.
U.S. NAVAL HISTORICAL CENTER PHOTO

Korean War Armistice Delegation, from left to right: Rear Admiral Arleigh A. Burke, USN; Major General Laurence C. Cragie, U.S. Air Force; Major General Paik Sun Yup, Republic of Korea Army; Vice Admiral C. Turner Joy, USN; Chief Delegate, General Ridgway, and Major Henry I. Hodes, U.S. Army; July 10, 1951.
OFFICIAL U.S. NAVY PHOTO

Below: An Ordnance Salvage Dump manned by Korean laborers unloading empty shell casings for salvage. 6 September 1951.
U.S. ARMY PHOTO

Right: SFC Carl W. Howard and PFC Daniel Wellman use Korean methods for transporting supplies.
U.S. ARMY PHOTO

Korean War
Medal of Honor Recipients

The Medal of Honor is the United States highest military honor. It is awarded for acts of bravery above and beyond the call of duty. The award is usually presented by the President of the United States at the White House in a ceremony intended to show the gratitude of the American people. Posthumous awards are presented to next of kin and are represented in the lists that follow by the letter **P**.

AIR FORCE

George A. Davis
Major, Sinuiju-Yalu River area, Korea, February 10, 1952, 334th Fighter Squadron, 4th Fighter Group, 5th Air Force
An experienced pilot, he was killed on his 59th combat mission protecting a squadron of bombers. **P**

Louis J. Sebille
Major, Hanchang, Korea, August 5, 1950, 67th Fighter-Bomber Squadron, 18th Fighter-Bomber Group, 5th Air Force
Killed after flying his aircraft into enemy troops. **P**

Charles J. Loring, Jr.
Major, Sniper Ridge, North Korea, November 22, 1952, 80th Fighter-Bomber Squadron, 8th Fighter-Bomber Wing
Killed when he flew his airplane into enemy gun emplacements. **P**

John S. Walmsley, Jr.
Captain, Yangdok,Korea, September 14, 1951, 8th Bombardment Squadron, 3d Bomb Group
Flew his plane through an intense enemy barrage to defend ground forces. **P**

ARMY

Stanley T. Adams
Sergeant, Sesim-ni, Korea, February 4, 1951, 19th Infantry Regiment
Led a bayonet charge against a numerically superior force.

Melvin L. Brown
Private First Class, Kasan, Korea, September 4, 1950, Company D, 8th Engineer Combat Battalion
Killed after single-handedly defended a section of wall until all of his ammunition was expended. P

Charles H. Barker
Private, Sokkogae, Korea, June 4, 1953, Company K, 17th Infantry Regiment, 7th Infantry Division
Voluntarily elected to maintain a defense and was last seen in close hand-to-hand combat with the enemy. P

Lloyd L. Burke
First Lieutenant, Chong-dong, Korea, October 28, 1951, Company G, 5th Cavalry Regiment, 1st Cavalry Division
Attacked the enemy in order to rescue his company who were pinned down.

Emory L. Bennett
Private First Class, Sobangsan, Korea, June 24, 1951, Company B, 15th Infantry Regiment, 3d Infantry Division
Killed while providing devastating covering fire for departing elements. P

Tony K. Burris
Sergeant First Class, Mundung-ni, Korea, October 8, 1951 to October 9, 1951, Company L, 38th Infantry Regiment, 2d Infantry Division
Destroyed multiple enemy positions and killed several of the enemy. P

David B. Bleak
Sergeant, Minari-gol, Korea, June 14, 1952, Medical Company 223d Infantry Regiment, 40th Infantry Division
Administered first aid to several wounded soldiers and killed several of the enemy in hand to hand combat.

Cornelius H. Charlton
Sergeant, Chipo-ri, Korea, June 2, 1951, Company C, 24th Infantry Regiment, 25th Infantry Division
Although wounded, single-handedly destroyed two Chinese positions. Killed by a grenade. P

Nelson V. Brittin
Sergeant First Class, Yonggong-ni, Korea, March 7, 1951, Company I, 19th Infantry Regiment
Killed 20 enemy soldiers and destroyed four automatic weapons to help his company advance into an enemy position. P

Gilbert G. Collier
Corporal, Tutayon, Korea, July 19, 1953 to July 20, 1953, Company F, 223d Infantry Regiment, 40th Infantry Division
Killed while remaining with his wounded commanding officer, killing two hostile soldiers and engaging in hand to hand combat. P

ARMY

John W. Collier
Corporal, Chindong-ni, Korea, September 19, 1950, Company C, 27th Infantry Regiment
Threw himself on a grenade to save fellow soldiers. P

Reginald B. Desiderio
Captain, Ipsok, Korea, November 27, 1950, Company E, 27th Infantry Regiment, 25th Infantry Division
Although wounded, he charged the enemy, inflicting many casualties and inspiring his troops. P

Samuel Streit Coursen
First Lieutenant, Kaesong, Korea, October 12, 1950, Company C, 5th Cavalry Regiment
Engaged the enemy in hand-to-hand combat in an effort to protect his wounded comrade until he himself was killed. P

Carl H. Dodd
Second Lieutenant, Subuk, Korea, January 30, 1951 to January 31, 1951, Company E, 5th Infantry Regiment, 24th Infantry Division
Attacked the enemy until he and his men successfully captured Hill 256.

Gordon M. Craig
Corporal, Kasan, Korea, September 10, 1950, Reconnaissance Company, 1st Cavalry Division
Sacrificed his life by smothering a grenade with his body. P

Ray E. Duke
Sergeant First Class, Mugok, Korea, April 26, 1951, Company C, 21st Infantry Regiment, 24th Infantry Division
Wounded and unable to walk, he urged his comrades to leave him to continue shooting at the enemy. P

Jerry K. Crump
Corporal, Chorwon, Korea, September 6, 1951 to September 7, 1951, Company L, 7th Infantry Regiment, 3d Infantry Division
Threw himself on a grenade, inspiring his comrades to a successful counter-attack.

Junior D. Edwards
Sergeant First Class, Changbong-ni, Korea, January 2, 1951, Company E, 23d Infantry Regiment, 2d Infantry Division
Killed after attacking the enemy multiple times, killing several. P

William F. Dean
Major General, Taejon, Korea, July 20, 1950 to July 21, 1950, 24th Infantry Division
Led his division in making a last stand at Taejon. Separated from his soldiers, he was wounded and taken as a POW for the rest of the war.

John Essebagger, Jr.
Corporal, Popsudong, Korea, April 25, 1951, Company A, 7th Infantry Regiment, 3d Infantry Division
Although they were outnumbered, he volunteered to remain to provide security for withdrawing squads. P

ARMY

Don C. Faith, Jr.
Lieutenant Colonel, Chosin Reservoir, Korea, November 27, 1950 to December 1, 1950, 1st Battalion, 32d Infantry Regiment, 7th Infantry Division
Repeatedly led his men in combat for five days until he was killed. P

Charles George
Private First Class, Songnae-dong, Korea, November 30, 1952, Company C, 179th Infantry Regiment, 45th Infantry Division, Native American Medal of Honor Recipient
Threw himself upon a grenade. P

Charles L. Gilliland
Private First Class, Tongmang-ni, Korea, April 25, 1951, Company I, 7th Infantry Regiment, 3d Infantry Division
Volunteered to remain to cover the withdrawal of his company and hold the enemy at bay. P

Clair Goodblood
Corporal, Popsu-dong, Korea, April 24, 1951 to April 25, 1951, Company D, 7th Infantry Regiment, Native American Medal of Honor
Killed after refusing medical aid and killing 100 enemy soldiers. P

Lester Hammond, Jr.
Corporal, Kumwha, Korea, August 14, 1952, Company A, 187th Airborne Regimental Combat Team
Coordinated and directed crippling fire on the enemy. P

Melvin O. Handrich
Master Sergeant, Sobuk San Mountain, Korea, August 25, 1950 to August 26, 1950, Company C, 5th Infantry Regiment
After being severely wounded he refused to be evacuated and continued to direct the company's fire. P

Jack G. Hanson
Private First Class, Pachi-dong, Korea, June 7, 1951, Company F, 31st Infantry Regiment
He was found with his empty pistol, a bloody machete and 22 enemy dead. P

Lee R. Hartell
First Lieutenant, Kobangsan-ni, Korea, August 27, 1951, Battery A, 15th Field Artillery Battalion, 2d Infantry Division
While in the line of fire, he made a final radio call urging friendly elements to fire continuously. P

Raymond Harvey
Captain, Taemi-Dong, Korea, March 9, 1951, Company C, 17th Infantry Regiment
He used carbine fire and grenades to sweep an enemy emplacement killing its 5 occupants.

Frederick F. Henry
First Lieutenant, Am-Dong, Korea, September 1, 1950, Company F, 38th Infantry Regiment
"Last seen single-handedly firing all available weapons causing 50 enemy casualties." P

ARMY

Rodolfo P. Hernandez
Corporal, Wontong-ni, Korea,
May 31, 1951, Company G,
187th Airborne Regimental
Combat Team
*Rushed the enemy, killing 6 before
falling unconscious from grenade,
bayonet, and bullet wounds.*

Billie G. Kanell
Private, Pyongyang, Korea, Sep-
tember 7, 1951, Company I, 35th
Infantry Regiment, 25th Infantry
Division
*He absorbed the blast of two gre-
nades with his body to protect 2 of
his comrades from injury.* P

Einar H. Ingman, Jr.
Corporal, Maltari, Korea, Febru-
ary 26, 1951, Company E, 17th
Infantry Regiment, 7th Infantry
Division
*As a result of his singular action the
defense of the enemy was broken.*

Father Emil Kapaun
Captain, US Army Chaplain
Corps, Pyoktong, North Korea,
May 23, 1951, 3rd Battalion, 8th
Cavalry
*At a POW camp, he mediated
disputes stole food for the sick and
raised morale.* P

William R. Jecelin
Sergeant, Saga, Korea, Septem-
ber 19, 1950, Company C, 35th
Infantry Regiment, 25th Infantry
Division
*He dived on the grenade, saving the
lives of the other American soldiers
but was killed in the blast.* P

Loren R. Kaufman
Sergeant First Class, Yongsan,
Korea, September 5, 1950, Com-
pany G, 9th Infantry Regiment
*Repeatedly attacked the enemy,
forcing them to retreat.*

Mack A. Jordan
Private First Class, Kumsong,
Korea, November 15, 1951,
Company K, 21st Infantry Regi-
ment, 24th Infantry Division
*Both legs were severed. Despite mor-
tal wounds, he continued to deliver
deadly fires.* P

Woodrow W. Keeble
Master Sergeant, Sangsan-ni,
Korea, October 20, 1951, Native
American Medal of Honor
*Single-handedly destroyed three
enemy machine-gun bunkers and
killed 7 enemy soldiers.* P

Anthony T. Kaho'ohanohano
Private First Class, near Chup'a-
ri, Korea, September 1, 1951,
Company H, 17th Infantry Regiment, 7th Infantry Division
*When his ammunition was
depleted, he fought in hand-to-hand
combat until he was killed.* P

Noah O. Knight
Private First Class, Kowang-San,
Korea, November 24, 1951,
Company F, 7th Infantry Regi-
ment, 3d Infantry Division
*Killed while attacking three enemy
troops attempting to place demoli-
tion charges.* P

Army

Ernest R. Kouma
Sergeant First Class, Agok, Korea, September 1, 1950, Company A, 72d Tank Battalion
Risked his life by attacking and killing at least 250 of the enemy.

Edward C. Krzyzowski
Captain, Tondul, Korea, September 3, 1951, Company B, 9th Infantry Regiment, 2d Infantry Division
Spearheaded an assault against strongly defended Hill 700. Killed by an enemy sniper. P

Darwin K. Kyle
Second Lieutenant, Kamil-ni, Korea, February 16, 1951, Company K, 7th Infantry Regiment, 3d Infantry Division
For repeated attacks against the enemy. Killed by a burst from an enemy submachine gun. P

Hubert L. Lee
Master Sergeant, Ip-ori, Korea, February 1, 1951, Company I, 23d Infantry Regiment, 2d Infantry Division
Although seriously wounded continued to lead his men and fight the enemy.

George D. Libby
Sergeant, Taejon, Korea, July 20, 1950, Company C, 3d Engineer Combat Battalion, 24th Infantry Division
Sacrificed his life to shield the driver of a rescue vehicle from enemy rounds. P

Charles R. Long
Sergeant, near Hoengseong, Korea, February 12, 1951, Company M, 38th Infantry Regiment, 2d Infantry Division
Remained in forward position to target the enemy with mortar fire until his position was surrounded. P

William F. Lyell
Corporal, Chup'a-ri, Korea, August 31, 1951, Company F, 17th Infantry Regiment, 7th Infantry Division
Fearlessly exposed himself to enemy fire, while directing and encouraging his men until he was killed. P

Benito Martinez
Corporal, Satae-ri, Korea, September 6, 1952, Company A, 27th Infantry Regiment, 25th Infantry Division
Refused to be rescued due to enemy troop activity and continued to fight the enemy until killed. P

Robert M. McGovern
First Lieutenant, Kamyangjan-ni, Korea, January 30, 1951, Company A, 5th Cavalry Regiment, 1st Cavalry Division
Killed by a burst of machine gun fire after destroying an enemy gun emplacement. P

Leroy A. Mendonca
Sergeant, Chich-on, Korea, July 4, 1951, Company B, 7th Infantry Regiment, 3d Infantry Division
Sacrificed his life by remaining in an exposed position and covering the platoon's withdrawal. P

ARMY

Lewis L. Millett
Captain, Soam-Ni, Korea, February 7, 1951, Company E, 27th Infantry Regiment
"Led a bayonet charge against the enemy."

John U. D. Page
Lieutenant Colonel, Battle of Chosin Reservoir, Korea, December 10, 1950, X Corps Artillery
Repeatedly attacked the enemy and defended his convoy until killed. P

Hiroshi H. Miyamura
Corporal, Taejon-ni, Korea, April 25, 1951, 3rd Infantry Division
First Medal of Honor to be classified Top Secret. This was because he was being held as a POW by the Communists.

Charles F. Pendleton
Corporal, Choo Gung-Dong, Korea, July 16, 1953 to July 17, 1953, Company D, 15th Infantry Regiment, 3d Infantry Division
Although wounded refused medical treatment and continued to fight the enemy until killed. P

Ola L. Mize
Surang-ni, Korea, June 11, 1953, Company K, 15th Infantry Regiment, 3d Infantry Division
Repeatedly risked his life to fight back the enemy and protect several wounded soldiers.

Herbert K. Pililaau
Private First Class, Pia-ri, Korea, September 17, 1951, Company C, 23d Infantry Regiment, 2nd Infantry Division
"Defeated more than 40 of the enemy." P

Donald R. Moyer
Sergeant First Class, Seoul, Korea, May 20, 1951, Company E, 35th Infantry Regiment
Sacrificed his life by smothering a grenade with his body. P

John A. Pittman
Sergeant, Kujangdong, Korea, November 26, 1950, Company C, 23d Infantry Regiment, 2d Infantry Division
Protected his squad by smothering a grenade with his body.

Joseph R. Ouellette
Private First Class, Yongsan, Korea, September 3, 1950, Company H, 9th Infantry Regiment, 2d Infantry Division
Repeatedly risked his life to gather grenades and ammunition until killed by enemy fire. P

Ralph E. Pomeroy
Private First Class, Kumhwa, Korea, October 15, 1952, Company E, 31st Infantry Regiment, 7th Infantry Division
Sacrificed his life manning a heavy machine gun until mortally wounded. P

ARMY

Donn F. Porter
Sergeant, Mundung-ni, Korea, September 7, 1952, Company G, 14th Infantry Regiment, 25th Infantry Division
Killed after fighting back a superior enemy force. P

Mitchell Red Cloud, Jr.
Corporal, Chonghyon, Korea, November 5, 1950, 24th Infantry Division Native American Medal of Honor
After being seriously wounded, continued to fight the enemy until he was killed. P

Joseph C. Rodriguez
Private First Class, Munye-ri, Korea, May 21, 1951, Company F, 17th Infantry Regiment, 7th Infantry Division
Single-handedly destroyed several enemy gun emplacements and foxholes.

Ronald E. Rosser
Corporal, Ponggilli, Korea, January 12, 1952, Heavy Mortar Company, 38th Infantry Regiment, 2d Infantry Division
Repeatedly risked his life to fight the enemy and rescue several wounded soldiers.

Tibor Rubin
Corporal, Korea, July 23, 1950 to April 20, 1953, Company I, 8th Cavalry Regiment, 1st Cavalry Division
For single-handedly defending his regiment during their retreat and saving the lives of fellow soldiers in a POW camp.

Daniel D. Schoonover
Corporal, Sokkogae, Korea, July 8, 1953 to July 10, 1953, Company A, 13th Engineer Combat Battalion, 7th Infantry Division
Last seen operating an automatic rifle with devastating effect until mortally wounded by artillery fire. P

Edward R. Schowalter, Jr.
First Lieutenant, Kumhwa, Korea, October 14, 1952, Company A, 31st Infantry Regiment, 7th Infantry Division
Although wounded, he continued to fight and lead his men until they defeated the enemy.

Richard Thomas Shea
First Lieutenant, Sokkogae, Korea, July 6, 1953 to July 8, 1953, Company A 17th Infantry Regiment, 7th Infantry Division
In over 18 hours of heavy fighting, he organized a successful defense single-handedly. P

William S. Sitman
Sergeant First Class, Chipyong-ni, Korea, February 14, 1951, Company M, 23d Infantry Regiment, 2d Infantry Division
Protected his squad by smothering a grenade with his body. P

David M. Smith
Private First Class, Yongsan, Korea, September 1, 1950, Company E, 9th Infantry Regiment, 2d Infantry Division
Pfc. Smith flung himself on a grenade and saved 5 men from death. P

ARMY

Clifton T. Speicher
Corporal, Minarigol, Korea, June 14, 1952, Company F, 223d Infantry Regiment, 40th Infantry Division
Died from wounds received after charging into an enemy machine gun nest. P

William Thompson
Private First Class, Haman, Korea, August 6, 1950, 24th Company M, 24th Infantry Regiment, 25th Infantry Division
Wounded, he refused to leave his position. His last words were "Get out of here, I'll cover you!" P

James L. Stone
First Lieutenant, Sokkogae, Korea, November 22, 1951, Company E 8th Cavalry Regiment, 1st Cavalry Division
Captured while leading his men against an overwhelming enemy assault.

Charles W. Turner
Sergeant First Class, Yongsan, Korea, September 1, 1950, 2d Reconnaissance Company, 2d Infantry Division
Used his tank to destroy seven enemy machine gun nests and covered his units' withdrawal until killed. P

Luther H. Story
Private First Class, Agok, Korea, September 1, 1950, Company A, 9th Infantry Regiment, 2d Infantry Division
Remained to cover the company's withdrawal. When last seen he was firing every weapon available. P

Travis E. Watkins
Master Sergeant, Yongsan, Korea, August 31, 1950 to September 3, 1950, Company H, 9th Infantry Regiment, 2d Infantry Division
Wounded and paralyzed from the waist down, he continued to encourage his men. P

Jerome A. Sudut
Second Lieutenant, Kumhwa, Korea, September 12, 1951, Company B, 27th Infantry Regiment, 25th Infantry Division
Though mortally wounded, he jumped into the emplacement and killed the remaining enemy soldier. P

Ernest E. West
Private First Class, Sataeri, Korea, October 12, 1952, Company L, 14th Infantry Regiment, 25th Infantry Division
Although wounded he assisted in evacuating the wounded and killed several of the enemy.

Henry Svehla
Private First Class, Korea, June 12, 1952, Company F, 32nd Infantry Regiment, 7th Infantry Division
"Without hesitation and undoubtedly aware of extreme danger, threw himself upon the grenade." P

Benjamin F. Wilson
Master Sergeant, Hwach'on-Myon, Korea, June 5, 1951, Company I, 31st Infantry Regiment, 7th Infantry Division
Repeatedly risked his life in order for his troops to reorganize and counterattack.

ARMY

Richard G. Wilson
Private First Class, Opari, Korea, October 21, 1950, Co. 1, Medical Company, 187th Airborne Infantry Regiment
Sacrificed his life to aid a fellow soldier shielding them from enemy fire with his own body. P

Bryant H. Womack
Private First Class, Sokso-ri, Korea, March 12, 1952, Medical Company, 14th Infantry Regiment, 25th Infantry Division
Sacrificed his life aiding other wounded soldiers. P

Robert H. Young
Private First Class, north of Kaesong, Korea, October 9, 1950, Company E, 8th Cavalry Regiment, 1st Cavalry Division
Although wounded, repeatedly repelled the enemy and insisted other wounded be treated first. P

MARINES

Charles G. Abrell
Corporal, Hangnyong, Korea, June 10, 1951, 2nd Battalion, 1st Marines, 1st Marine Division
Hurled himself into an enemy bunker with a live grenade stopping accurate and fatal fire on his unit. P

Stanley R. Christianson
Private First Class, Seoul, Korea, September 29, 1950, Company E, 2nd Battalion, 1st Marines, 1st Marine Division (Rein.)
Remained in his position firing at oncoming hostile troops until he was overrun and killed. P

William E. Barber
Captain, Battle of Chosin Reservoir, Korea, November 28, 1950 to December 2, 1950, Company F, 2nd Battalion, 7th Marines, 1st Marine Division
Risked his life as a commanding officer in action against enemy forces.

Henry A. Commiskey, Sr.
Second Lieutenant, Yongdungp'o, Korea, September 20, 1950, Company C, 1st Battalion, 1st Marines, 1st Marine Division (Rein.)
Attacked the enemy, killing several and inflicting significant damage.

William B. Baugh
Private, Koto-ri to Hagaru-ri, Korea, November 29, 1950, Company G, 3d Battalion, 1st Marine Division (Rein.)
Killed when he risked his life to save his fellow Marines during a nighttime enemy attack. P

Jack A. Davenport
Corporal, Songnae-Dong, Korea, September 21, 1951, Company G, 3rd Battalion, 5th Marines, 1st Marine Division (Rein.)
Smothered the explosion of a grenade with his body in order to save the life of his fellow Marine. P

Hector A. Cafferata, Jr.
Private, Chosin Reservoir, Korea, November 28, 1950, Company F, 2nd Battalion, 7th Marines, 1st Marine Division (Rein.)
Single handedly fought off an enemy attack.

Ray Davis
Lieutenant Colonel, Hagaru-ri, Korea, December 1 to December 4, 1950, 1st Battalion, 7th Marines, 1st Marine Division (Rein.)
During the Battle of the Chosin Reservoir led his battalion in fierce firefights with the Chinese army.

David B. Champagne
Corporal, Korea, May 28, 1952, Company A, 1st Battalion, 7th Marines, 1st Marine Division (Rein.)
Saved members of his fire team by throwing an enemy grenade out of a trench. P

Duane E. Dewey
Corporal, Panmunjon, Korea, April 16, 1952, Company E, 2nd Battalion, 5th Marines, 1st Marine Division (Rein.)
While being treated by a Navy medical corpsman, flung himself onto a grenade, saving the corpsman and several Marines.

Marines

Fernando Luis García
Private First Class, Korea, September 5, 1952, Company I, 3rd Battalion, 5th Marines, 1st Marine Division (Rein.)
Threw his body upon a hostile grenade, saving the life of another Marine. P

Robert S. Kennemore
Staff sergeant, north of Yudam-ni, Korea, November 28, 1950, Company E, 2nd Battalion, 7th Marines 1st Marine Division (Rein.)
Deliberately covered an enemy grenade with his foot to keep his men from being wounded or killed.

Edward Gomez
Private First Class, Hill 749, Korea, September 14, 1951, Company E, 2nd Battalion, 1st Marines, 1st Marine Division (Rein.)
Killed when he dove into a ditch with a live grenade, saving other Marines. P

John D. Kelly
Private First Class, Korea, May 28, 1952, Company C, 1st Battalion, 7th Marines 1st Marine Division (Rein.)
Killed while attacking and destroying several enemy bunkers single-handedly. P

Ambrosio Guillen
Staff Sargeant, Songuch-on, Korea, July 25, 1953, Company F, 2nd Battalion, 7th Marines, 1st Marine Division (Rein.)
Killed while exposing himself to attacks in defense of the position and the evacuation of the wounded. P

Herbert A. Littleton
Private First Class, Chungchon, Korea, April 22, 1951, Company C, 1st Battalion, 7th Marines 1st Marine Division (Rein.)
Sacrificed his life by smothering a grenade with his body. P

James E. Johnson
Sergeant, Yudam-ni, Korea, December 2, 1950, Company J, 3rd Battalion, 7th Marines 1st Marine Division (REIN)
Although seriously wounded, was last seen fighting the enemy in hand to hand combat. P

Baldomero Lopez
First Lieutenant, Battle of Inchon, Korea, September 15, 1950, Company A, 1st Battalion, 5th Marines 1st Marine Division (Rein.)
Smothered a hand grenade with his own body. P

Jack W. Kelso
Private First Class, Korea, Oct. 2, 1952, 3rd Battalion, 7th Marines, 1st Marine Division (Rein.)
Killed while providing cover fire for several Marines pinned down in a bunker, allowing them to escape. P

Daniel P. Matthews
Sergeant, Vegas Hill, Korea, March 28, 1953, Company F, 2nd Battalion, 7th Marines, 1st Marine Division (Rein.)
Sacrificed his life to silence an enemy gun emplacement. P

Marines

Frederick W. Mausert, III
Sergeant, Songnap-yong, Korea, September 12, 1951, Company B, 1st Battalion, 7th Marines, 1st Marine Division (Rein.)
While severely wounded, single-handedly defeated an enemy gun emplacement and drew enemy fire. P

Raymond G. Murphy
Second Lieutenant, Korea, February 3, 1953, Company A, 1st Battalion, 5th Marines, 1st Marine Division (Rein.)
Wounded twice, refused treatment until all his men preceded him in departing to the main lines.

Alford L. McLaughlin
Private First Class, Korea, September 4, 1952, Company L, 3rd Battalion, 5th Marines, 1st Marine Division (Rein.)
Although painfully wounded, he fought off the enemy until they were defeated.

Reginald R. Myers
Major, Hagaru-ri, Korea, November 29, 1950, 3d Battalion, 1st Marines, 1st Marine Division (Rein.)
During subzero temperatures, led his unit in an attack which killed 600 enemies and wounded 500.

Frank N. Mitchell
First Lieutenant, Hansan-ni, Korea, November 26, 1950, Company A, 1st Battalion, 7th Marines, 1st Marine Division (Rein.)
Killed by a burst of small arms fire after single-handedly covering his squad's escape. P

Eugene A. Obregon
Private First Class, Seoul, Korea, September 26, 1950, Company G, 3rd Battalion, 5th Marines, 1st Marine Division (Rein.)
Used his body as a shield to protect another wounded Marine. P

Walter C. Monegan, Jr.
Private First Class, Sosa-ri, Korea, September 17, 1950 and September 20, 1950, Company F, 2nd Battalion, 1st Marines, 1st Marine Division (Rein.)
Killed while repeatedly attacking the enemy at night. P

George H. O'Brien, Jr.
Marine Corps, Second Lieutenant, Korea, October 27, 1952, Company H, 3rd Battalion, 7th Marines, 1st Marine Division (Rein.)
Provided cover and care for wounded while his unit was attacking the enemy.

Whitt L. Moreland
Private First Class, Kwagch'i-Dong, Korea, May 29, 1951, Company C, 1st Battalion, 5th Marines, 1st Marine Division (Rein.)
Sacrificed his life by smothering a grenade with his body. P

Lee H. Phillips
Corporal, Korea, November 4, 1950, Company E, 2nd Battalion, 7th Marines, 1st Marine Division (Rein.)
Risked his life to defeat a pocket of enemy resistance.

MARINES

James I. Poynter

Sergeant, Sudong, Korea, November 4, 1950, Company A, 1st Battalion, 7th Marines, 1st Marine Division (Rein.)
Sacrificed his life to kill several of the enemy with hand grenades to save a group of fellow Marines. P

George H. Ramer

Second Lieutenant, Korea, September 12, 1951, Company I, 3rd Battalion, 7th Marines, 1st Marine Division (Rein.)
Although wounded, led his men against superior force until his postion was overrun. P

Robert D. Reem

Second Lieutenant, Chinhung-ni, Korea, November 6, 1950, Company H, 3rd Battalion, 7th Marines, 1st Marine Division (Rein.)
Killed after he covered a grenade with his body. P

William E. Shuck, Jr.

Staff sergeant, Korea, July 3, 1952, Company G, 3rd Battalion, 7th Marines, 1st Marine Division (Rein.)
Sacrificed his life to assure that all dead and wounded were evacuated. P

Robert E. Simanek

Private First Class, Korea, August 17, 1952, Company F, 2nd Battalion, 5th Marines, 1st Marine Division (Rein.)
Risked his life to save his comrades by smothering a grenade with his body.

Carl L. Sitter

Marine Corps, Captain, Hagaru-ri, Korea, November 29, 1950 to November 30th
Although wounded, he refused to be evacuated and continued to fight until defense of the area was assured.

Sherrod E. Skinner, Jr.

Second Lieutenant, Korea, October 26, 1952, Battery F, 2nd Battalion, 11th Marines, 1st Marine Division (Rein.)
Fought off an enemy force for three hours and then sacrificed his life by smothering a grenade with his body. P

Archie Van Winkle

Staff sergeant, Sudong, Korea, November 2, 1950, Company B, 1st Battalion, 7th Marines, 1st Marine Division (Rein.)
Although severely wounded, he continued to fight and lead his men until he passed out from loss of blood.

Joseph Vittori

Corporal, Hill 749, Korea, September 15, 1951, Company F, 2nd Battalion, 1st Marines, 1st Marine Division (Rein.)
Killed while defending a sector where 200 enemy dead were found the following morning. P

Lewis G. Watkins

Staff sergeant, Korea, October 7, 1952, Company I, 3rd Battalion, 7th Marines, 1st Marine Division (Rein.)
Killed by an enemy grenade when it exploded in his hand. P

Marines

Harold E. Wilson
Technical Sergeant, Korea,
April 23, 1951 toApril 24, 1951,
Company G, 3rd Battalion, 1st
Marines, 1st Marine Division
(Rein.)
*Served in World War II, Korea and
Vietnam War; In addition to the
Medal of Honor he received five
purple hearts.*

William G. Windrich
Marine Corps, Staff sergeant,
Yudam-ni, Korea, December 1,
1950, Company I, 3rd Battalion,
5th Marines, 1st Marine Division
(Rein.)
*Sacrificed his life to direct his
men and rescue several wounded
Marines from a hillside.* P

NAVY

Edward C. Benfold
Corpsman Third Class, Korea, September 5, 1952, 1st Marine Division
Died while treating wounds and saving the lives of wounded Marines. P

William R. Charette
Hospital Corpsman Third Class, Vegas Hill, Korea, March 27, 1953, Company F, 2nd Battalion, 7th Marines, 1st Marine Division
Aided fellow soldiers under heavy fire.

Richard De Wert
Hospital man, Korea, April 5, 1951, 1st Marine Division (Rein.)
Died while treating wounds and saving the lives of wounded Marines. P

Francis C. Hammond
Hospital man, Korea, March 26, 1953 to March 27, 1953, 1st Battalion, 5th Marines, 1st Marine Division
Treated and directed the care of the wounded until he was struck by a round of enemy mortar fire and killed. P

Thomas J. Hudner, Jr.
Lieutenant, Junior Grade, Chosin Reservoir, Korea, December 4, 1950, Fighter Squadron 32, attached to U.S.S. Leyte
Crash landed his plane in the Chosin Reservoir to attempt to save squadron mate, Ensign Jesse Brown, first African-American naval aviator.

John E. Kilmer
Hospital man, Korea, August 13, 1952, 3rd Battalion, 7th Marines, 1st Marine Division
Killed while shielding a wounded man with his body. P

John K. Koelsch
Lieutenant, Junior Grade, Korea, July 3, 1951, Navy helicopter rescue unit
Died as a POW, after rescuing several crewmen from a downed helicopter. He evaded the enemy for nine days before being captured. P

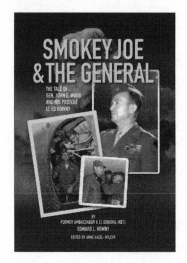

SMOKEY JOE & THE GENERAL

is the autobiographical account of Edward L. Rowny as a young West Point graduate embarking upon a remarkable life journey under the guidance and inspiration of eccentric but brilliant General John E. Wood.

Praise for *Smokey Joe & the General*:

"The remarkable General Edward Rowny has written the story his superior career entails. This is a wonderful account of service, intrigue, and military accomplishments of the highest degree. Page by page it takes the reader through a series of events that are in many senses spellbinding. A terrific read. Highly recommended."

— Television personality **Larry King**

"General Ed Rowny knows about many things; especially selfless service, integrity, and leadership. Thus his rich, nuanced and modest memoir is at the same time a valuable treatise on principled leadership as learned from General John E. Wood, Rowny's long-time mentor. It is a great story, begun in days of the Old Army but with much to teach those serving today and tomorrow."

— **Lewis Sorley**, author of Pulitzer Prize nominated *A Better War*

"Smokey Joe and the General is no ordinary military memoir. It covers the story of an astonishingly varied career that includes service in the combat engineers, commander of an infantry division, pioneering in the new techniques of armed helicopters, and finally Military Representative to the SALT Treaty with the Russians. Throughout this odyssey the General never forgets his first boss and mentor, Colonel "Smokey Joe" Wood. Written informally with plenty of humor and wisdom, Ed Rowny's book is both fascinating and informative".

— **John Eisenhower**, son of President Dwight D. Eisenhower, Brigadier General U.S. Army (ret.) & former Ambassador to Belgium

Available from Amazon.com in both print and Kindle versions.

Made in the USA
San Bernardino, CA
23 April 2017